STUDY SMART
SCORE HIGH

STUDY SMART SCORE HIGH
An innovative guide to learning effectively and staying ahead

Cedric M. Kenny

Sterling Paperbacks

STERLING PAPERBACKS
An imprint of
Sterling Publishers (P) Ltd.
A-59, Okhla Industrial Area, Phase-II,
New Delhi-110020.
Tel: 26387070, 26386209; Fax: 91-11-26383788
E-mail: mail@sterlingpublishers.com
ghai@nde.vsnl.net.in
www.sterlingpublishers.com

Study Smart Score High
© 2008, Cedric M. Kenny
ISBN 978 81 207 4087 7
Reprint 2009

The author and publisher specifically disclaim any liability, loss or risk, whatsoever, personal, or otherwise, which is incurred as a consequence, directly, or indirectly of the use and application of any of the contents of this book.

All rights are reserved.
No part of this publication may be reproduced, stored in a retrieval system or transmitted, in any form or by any means, mechanical, photocopying, recording or otherwise, without prior written permission of the original publisher.

Printed in India

Printed and Published by Sterling Publishers Pvt. Ltd., New Delhi-110 020.

For

Shobha, Payal and Varun

Acknowledgements

I have a number of people to thank whose encouragement and support gave shape to this book.

At the top of the list is my associate, Shobha Arora. She is the founder and principal of *Tender Feet Nursery School*, Nizamuddin East, New Delhi. Hers is a passionate lifestyle, which begins and ends each day in the midst of toddlers. Shobha Arora has the gift to connect with children instantly. Her natural flair for the arts coupled with an abundance of love for children and a deep understanding of effective parenting skills, stimulates all the toddlers, along with their parents and grandparents, to put their best foot forward with ease and joy. Working in this joyful environment at *Tender Feet* since 1983, has enabled me to shape many concepts which you will read about. Most of the theories contained in this book are borrowed lavishly from *Tender Feet*.

I thank Neena Malhotra who gave me the opportunity to work with pre-teens and teens in New Delhi. In 1984, Neena not only enlisted her son into my class but also knocked on the doors of her friends to form a bi-weekly study group. While her son was a brilliant student, others needed to be motivated. The *Tender Feet* stimuli initiated by Shobha Arora, was modified to suit the age and temperament of the pre-teens and teens. The modified alchemy worked wonders. In a matter of weeks, pre-teens and teens, not only changed their lifestyle habits but also improved their grades. The contents of this book unravel the alchemy of success pre-teens and teens have imbibed since 1984.

I thank Dr. Rajeev Sharma, Associate Professor, Ravi J. Mathai Centre of Education Innovation, Indian Institute of Management (IIM) – Ahmedabad, for prodding me to write this book. When Dr. Rajeev Sharma heard of my work with pre-teens and teens he was intrigued. With a lot of regret I had to decline his spontaneous offer to conduct research and write this book at the IIM – Ahmedabad. When I told him I was busy with work in New Delhi, he made a passionate plea of how thousands of students, parents and teachers, throughout the country, would gain by reading about such inspirational ways of self-improvement. Indeed, it is a privilege to know and be influenced by Dr. Rajeev Sharma.

I thank Gulraj Shahpuri, CEO and director of *Promise*, New Delhi who has so much faith in my educational and counselling concepts and theories. Gulraj Shahpuri is very hardworking and deeply committed about the holistic development of pre-teens and teens. His institution, *Promise* provides a roadmap for students and acts as a guidance system to enhance grades, attitudes and personality through improved habits. I am deeply touched to hear from many parents that Gulraj Shahpuri attributes to me the concepts his institution teaches.

A very special note of thanks to the parents and grandparents at *Tender Feet,* who have showered me with their love and trust. They hold the belief that I have the ability to show them the light and guide the destinies of their children. This book, without them, would never have seen the light of day.

Cedric M. Kenny

Prologue

Addressing a PTA at one of New Delhi's city schools on the topic *All Children Are Born Intelligent,* I concluded the first part of my interactive discourse by elaborating on a simile. I asked my audience, consisting of parents, teachers and the school management, to hold a hand forward and look at it closely. The thumb is placed way down from the four fingers. Each of the fingers is similar and yet has dissimilarities. Some are shapely, some stubby. We do not criticise the thumb and compare it to the size of the other fingers. Each of the five fingers plays a very important role in the overall functioning of the hand. In fact, anthropologists tell us that among the many tell-tale signs that differentiate primates from *homo sapiens,* is the use of the thumb and forefinger in picking objects. Primates are unable to do that. We never compare one finger with the other or fault our hand for holding up five un-uniformed fingers, but we compare some students with other students in class and fault them for not being better than others or as clever as others.

"Any questions?" I asked my audience. Someone stirred. "Yes, I would like to make a point," said a gentleman as he rose from his seat in the third row. "In every class there are dullards, average kids and there are brilliant ones. Students are graded by the quality of their performance. Their performance depends on the intelligence they possess." Having made his point, he looked around at the audience. As he sat down, there was a look of approval on the faces of the management, teachers and parents in the school hall. No one opposed his view. There it was, out in the open; home and school approving the existence of the academic caste

PROLOGUE ix

system among students – the brilliant, the average and the dull ones.

It is so easy to segregate kids, put them in compartments and hammer caste labels on those boxes. Are kids born average, dull or brilliant? If you take a look at newborn infants lying in rows of cots in the hospital nursery, would you point a finger at one infant and say, "Look, that's a dull one." Or, "See, over there, that one looks brilliant." No, we do not go about hammering labels on cots. All the infants look 'normal' because they are normal babies. Yet sadly, a few years later, when they go to school, many of these 'normal' kids will crack down under academic pressure. They will be labelled as average, intelligent or dullards. "Why does that happen?" you may want to know. "Can we pre-empt that breakdown?" I firmly believe you can pre-empt the breakdown. *Study Smart Score High* is the book with ready answers to pre-empt breakdowns and burnouts. Students with a high IQ but low EQ (emotional quotient) or SQ (social quotient) will gain as much as students who find it tedious to read, understand, memorise or write with difficulty. You will have to make the effort to guide them through the pages of this book.

What parent or educator would not want to use effective tools to bring respite to students weighed under the burden of academics? "Give me a lever long enough and I will move the world," said Archimedes. *Study Smart Score High* is the lever our students need to succeed. Use this book as your personal lever to de-stress students; the result will be two-fold: (a) it will infuse joy in children and (b) it will diffuse some of the pressure off academics. The book offers easy-to-follow instructions to suit all temperaments, showing methods to rev up the study engine and smoothly change gears – from being an average student to becoming an achiever, and from an achiever to climb higher and become a super achiever. *Study Smart Score High*, offers practical guidelines to students to:

    (a) overcome shortcomings by unleashing the powers of the mind;

    (b) develop positive belief in their abilities;

(c) structure their life to embrace habits of discipline; and

(d) become messengers of happiness.

The guidelines contained in this book, if read hurriedly and then put aside, will serve no purpose. On the other hand, when these guidelines are read carefully, assimilated and put to practice, they will boost confidence, motivate and ignite intelligence. Students will not only taste success in their academic endeavours but also will learn ways to live lives full of joy and happiness. Indeed, they will develop leadership skills to last a lifetime.

This book is addressed to parents, educators and students. Though the purpose of this book is to show students how to 'study smart and score high,' without proper direction from parents and teachers, their efforts may come to naught. Many parents and teachers may need to change their personal habits so that students are channelled better. Students will benefit immensely from the ideas researched in this book, when home and school work together, hand-in-hand to stimulate students to explore their full potential. Without positive support from parents and teachers, schooling will remain a tedious struggle.

Contents

	Acknowledgements	vi
	Prologue	viii
1.	Fine-tune Your Study Engine with Good Habits	1
2.	Distractions are Roadblocks to Success	9
3.	If You Listened Better, Wouldn't You Learn More?	17
4.	Why Throttle Untapped Potential?	25
5.	Don't Get Rundown by Stress	36
6.	Positive Juices Stimulate the Brain	48
7.	Homework is *Not* Injurious to Health	58
8.	Study Smart and Get to a Flying Start	66
9.	What is Reading without Understanding and Remembering?	77
10.	Accelerate Your Study Engine with Music	87
	Epilogue	96

1

Fine-tune Your Study Engine with Good Habits

Salient Features

We begin the odyssey by de-mystifying the myth that some are born intelligent, while others are born less intelligent. School grading indicates that low grades are synonymous with low intelligence and high grades are synonymous with high intelligence. You will soon realise that succeeding or failing has nothing to do with intelligence; instead, it has everything to do with habits. All of us are creatures of habit. Habits get ingrained in us through personal upbringing and lifestyles. As the case studies point out, children who are brought up on a diet of conveniences and inconsistencies will display habits of convenience rather than habits of discipline. Over a period of time, habits become characteristic of an individual's personality. Slothful habits pull down students, while habits of discipline help them to soar high. Why remain enslaved to slothful habits when you can ignite your intelligence through good habits? Success is yours if you choose to fine-tune your study engine using the lever of good habits.

Barring any genetic or neurological *mis*-wiring in the brain, or some genetic handicaps that may cause a slow-down in motor skills or in speaking, reading and writing, I believe that all humans are born equally intelligent. I will not go into the problems faced by autistic, bipolar, dyslexic, ADHD and the plight of those children who suffer from learning disorders. In this chapter, let us de-mystify an age-old belief which avers that people are not born equally intelligent. All through our lives we have accepted that IQ tests and school and college exams determine a student's academic aptitude and that low marks are synonymous with low intelligence, and high marks are synonymous with high intelligence. It is an error to link aptitude with intelligence. Academic aptitude has a lot to do with habits. Your success or failure is directly linked to your personal habits. By linking low aptitude to low intelligence, there is precious little you can do to enhance intelligence. On the contrary, there is everything you can do in your power to change habits that pull you down. There is no need to work hard. You need to work smart. If you change the course of your thoughts and change your habits, you can change failure into success.

We are Creatures of Habit

What separates high achievers from low achievers is not intelligence, but *habits* that govern our day-to-day activities. We are all creatures of habits. Some habits pull us down while some habits help us soar high. Some habits are born out of discipline while some habits are born our of convenience. Usually, habits that pull us down are habits of convenience and creature comforts, while habits that help us soar high are born by habits of discipline.

Toddlers who are fed on a diet of television will habitually sit in front of a television when they grow up to be young adults. And toddlers who are fed on a diet of varied activities like group-play, drawing, colouring, play-dough, nature walks, picture reading, yoga, aerobics, role play, *et al.*, will habitually look for creative opportunities to absorb their varied interests when they grow up to be adults. Let us take a good look at the people around us; there are family members, relatives, friends, acquaintances and strangers. We remember them by their characteristic actions that they perform habitually. They display a variety of diverse character traits. Some are happy, enthusiastic people while some are whiners and cribbers. Some bathe daily while some bathe irregularly. Some are at pains to look well-groomed, while some look dishevelled and are not bothered about it. Some eat at fixed times, while some eat outside mealtimes. Some are always punctual and some are always late. Some people keep their washrooms and other places impeccably clean while some leave them messy. Some people are gentle, caring and concerned, while some are cold, heartless and indifferent. Some people are polite and some are rude. Some are humble while some are pompous. Some are hardworking and industrious and some are lazy. The only thing they all have in common is that they are governed by their habits.

We become so much our habits that our family members, relatives and friends identify us by our habits. Our habits become our characteristic traits, which make us 'predictable' to people we live with or who happen to know us closely because we automatically behave the way we habitually do. Our habits become so ingrained in our psyche that our actions, accelerated by habits, shift to 'auto mode' in a blur of ease.

Habits get ingrained through upbringing

As young adults, whether they will be driven by a force of habits born out of convenience or by habits born out of discipline, will depend entirely on the lifestyle which they inherited in their formative years. You may not realise, but your lifestyle habits and attitudes impact the child's emotional and intellectual development. If you are tensed, pressured or stressed at home, at office or elsewhere, this stress finds its outlet in your speech, actions and behaviour and it affects the child. He grows up as an insecure and confused person. On the other hand, if you are content, relaxed and happy, this joyous attitude impacts your child's brain cells and he grows up as a happy, content and enthusiastic person. As parents, it is you who will create the primary environment for your child, not the neighbourhood. Children learn from their parents before they learn from their neighbours.

Eva D'Costa said, her twelve-year-old son, Sylvester, was obstinate, disobedient and turned a deaf ear to any advice. "He never listens," she said despondently. She blamed the neighbourhood children, television, his friends in school and the teachers for his negative behaviour. While counselling her, I told her to look back and recall the time when Sylvester was a toddler and recall moments when she called out to him and he ignored her. How she had coped with those responses in the past played a very important role in the present. Eva D'Costa confessed that she and her husband argued a lot in the presence of their child. Hearing his parents argue and quarrel, the child simply was not in the habit of listening to them. If spouses have divergent views on child upbringing, it is only natural that children will take them for granted and not listen because they are not in the habit of obeying any one.

On the other hand, Sudhir and Malthi made it a point to discuss their disagreements "never in Radha's presence." Even through their disagreements, they supported each other when they dealt with their daughter. Malthi never raised her voice because she never had to. Being nurtured in this environment, Radha automatically responded instantly to her parents commands. When she grew up to be a teenager, Radha obeyed her parents because she was in the habit of listening to them.

Do your pre-teens or teens hide or skip doing homework? Instead of shouting at them, find out what causes such behaviour. You may find that fussy eaters and study procrastinators have a lot in common. They share strong likes and dislikes. Try and recall the times when as a toddler your child wasted food on his plate because he found it unpleasant or distasteful. If you threw the food away or ate the leftovers, he expects you (now that he's a pre-teen or teen) to handle his homework which he finds distasteful or unpleasant. Conversely, toddlers who polished off their plates of food because their parents had a natural knack of putting small portions of food which the child could finish and then ask for more, those same kids as pre-teens and teens, handled their homework responsibly on their own. Have you noticed that generally children with a strong dislike for certain foods also do poorly in certain subjects? In many cases, you will see some children reject food instantly without tasting it saying, "I don't like it," or "I hate this food." It is important for parents to develop the taste buds of children at a very early age so that they can (a) savour and enjoy a variety of foods and (b) are more accommodating and less wilful. When you break down mental blocks at an early age, children not only enjoy all types of foods but also happily participate in a variety of activities, games and studies.

While on the subject of instilling study habits in children, I would like to share Shaihira Hussain's example. This mother recalls how she had dealt with her teenager's study habits when he was barely five years old.

When Haneef was five years old, Shaihira remembered she would open his school bag while he ate his lunch. She would go through his books to see if he had brought homework from school. On 'discovering' there was homework, Shaihira would express delight and interest in it. She would ask him about what had happened in school while he ate lunch. She had to make sure that Haneef knew his job was to study, and his experiences each day in school were just as worthy of discussion as her and her husband's were. Shaihira routinely set post-lunch hours as homework time. On days when there was no homework, she read to Haneef and played educational games of some kind. The key value she ingrained in Haneef was that post-lunch hours were dedicated to learning and not to television, computer games, playing outside or lazing around. Having set the study routine, Haneef never forgot to do his homework even as a teenager. By force of habit, he automatically opened his school bag after lunch and spent his time at the study desk.

Are you among those parents who complain that their teens generally are bored, with no interests or hobbies? Many parents, teachers and principals of schools focus solely on academics, believing that mastering academics is the one and only goal the child should have. Or, are you among those parents who believe that hobbies too are important? If hobbies are important, are you prepared to provide a 'support system' for your children to pursue hobbies? Allowing children to indulge in hobbies requires parents to spend a lot more time with their children. For instance, you will have to scout around, make inquiries, visit different activity centres to check out what's available and its suitability to your child's age, school schedule and its overall usefulness. All this is time consuming. After you have made your choice, you have to arrange for reliable transportation to ferry your kids back and forth for the entire duration of the activity that may consume you for a few weeks, months, or years. If this will stress you out, you are wasting your time, money and energy because you will pass the stress to the children and they will never enjoy those activities; they will find faults with the instructors or the programmes.

Are you among those parents who whine and complain about children hooked on to television? Why nag the kids when they are in their teens. Look at the way you handled them when they were toddlers. Do you remember the times when those teens were toddlers and how they were kept occupied. Did you succumb to pester power? If they kept pestering, did you snap at them, cuff them, or did you give in and switch on the television? If they took forever to finish their meals or were restless at the dining table, did you put on the television? When you were too tired to read to them, did you put on the television? When you were too busy to play with them, did you put on the television? When you went out shopping, did you put on the television? If you had to attend a night party, did you put on the television? The days they were sick and were unable to attend school, did you put on the television to keep them in bed? If you chose television as your babysitter, then your overdependence on the electronic babysitter has stunted the child's emotional and intellectual development. The television is one such example; it could be *ayahs*, toys, computers, electronic games, foods, pets or some other distraction instead of the television.

Life is About Choices, Not Chances

Avantika Rathore appeared to have an easygoing air about her. She was twenty-nine and a mother of a four-year-old son. Her paediatrician had advised her to seek counsel from a child psychiatrist on how to discipline her child. After she met the child psychiatrist, she knocked on my door. She seemed troubled about the doctor's recommendation but tried to mask her anxiety. She confessed that she didn't believe in "disciplining kids because there are no guarantees in life that children will grow up to meet the parents' expectations." She further added, "I have no expectations of Avinash; if I don't have expectations, I won't be hurt." Was Avantika Rathore afraid of getting hurt or was she hurting already, I wondered? She then enumerated Avinash's fits of rage and the temper tantrums he threw, his acts of defiance and the demands he made. I pointed out to Avantika Rathore the difference between living for the future and living in the present. You cannot leave parenting to chance; you have to take a stand. While the future is loaded with expectations, the present is loaded with choices. To live in the present, Avantika Rathore would have to make a choice between nurturing a dependent child or an independent one. If she chose to nurture a child who would grow up to be emotionally independent then she would need to alter her personal lifestyle and habits before she attempted to modify her child's behaviour. On the other hand, if Avantika Rathore chose to allow Avinash to grow emotionally dependent, then she would not need to alter her current lifestyle or her personal habits.

Playing God

You are the God who moulds children in your own image and likeness. As parents, you are the ones responsible for the upbringing of your children. In the final analysis, it's all up to you – how you want to raise your kids. You may want to raise kids who will grow up to be independent or you may want to raise kids who will remain dependent. "It's all about stimuli and response," say psychologists; while the folks on the farm would say, "What you sow is what you reap." The choice is yours; after all, by the time the child grows up to be a young adult at twenty, he will function on 'auto-mode.' Don't grudge him his habits if they annoy you. His actions will flow effortlessly from the life-script you assisted him with, to map on his brain cells since he was a toddler. Indeed, a daunting thought on how your personal habits influence your children's thoughts, attitudes and lifestyles.

Points to Remember

1. If your performance is average or below average, it has nothing to do with low intelligence. It is to do with your personal habits. Discipline yourself to become high achievers.
2. Habits of convenience pull you down while habits of discipline pull you up.
3. Personal habits get ingrained through lifestyle and upbringing.
4. Your behaviour becomes your personality. Life is not about chances; choose the person you want to be and structure your behaviour accordingly.
5. Children grow up in the image and likeness of parents. What you sow is what you reap.

2

Distractions are Roadblocks to Success

Salient Features

Parents and teachers often complain that students get distracted easily. To understand the problem, take a look at the profiles of three individuals attending a seminar. In this case study, you will see how individual lifestyle habits influenced their participation at the seminar. One was a daydreamer, the second lacked total focus and the third participated with single-minded intensity. By identifying the causes of distraction, you can overcome them. Here are five remedies to overcome five problems that cause distractions. 1) Physical Restlessness: Voluntary and involuntary body movements distract your attention and cause you to lose concentration. 2) Mental Restlessness: You 'pretend' to listen attentively while your mind is miles away from the speaker. 3) Interruption: You interrupt the speaker, at times even before the sentence is over. When you do so, your ears automatically stop registering what the speaker said. 4) Weak Sleep Drive: Those with erratic sleep patterns usually display poor attention, high irritability and low concentration levels. You need to guard your sleep habits. Your success depends on how well you snooze for at least eight hours every night. 5) Avoiding Eye Contact: Where the eyes go, the ears follow. If you do not lock your eyes with the eyes of the speaker, your mind and body will take you away from your main objective. Control your eye movement and you will control distractions.

There are high achievers and there are low achievers. The low achievers believe they are going through a phase that is 'unlucky.' They believe they are trapped by circumstances. They wish they were blessed with the kind of luck that favours others so that they, too, could be high achievers. But, it is not luck; instead, you will see that people who are high achievers are attentive and focused, while people who are low achievers are distracted, restless and inattentive. The following case study will help you analyse in depth the profiles of both types.

Case Study

Sudhanshu Aggarwal, at thirty-four was an exporter of costume jewellery. His wife and three children lived comfortably in an up-market apartment in New Delhi. Sudhanshu met me to discuss his problem. Two business friends, Shivang Misra and Ehsaas Pandey coaxed Sudhanshu to attend a one-day seminar on *Evolving Entrepreneurship* conducted by a top-notch guru from the UK. Sudhanshu paid thirty-five thousand rupees as seminar fee. At the seminar, within ten minutes of the speaker having warmed up to the subject, Sudhanshu went off a tangent and began to daydream. His mind got cluttered with mixed thoughts which distracted him from concentrating on the speaker. A sudden burst of laughter in the audience brought Sudhanshu back to the seminar. He asked his friend, Ehsaas Pandey, sitting to his left, about the joke he missed. As she related the episode, the audience guffawed louder, and she stopped mid-sentence to focus on the speaker. Sudhanshu turned to his right. Shivang Misra, was busy taking down notes. He asked Misra about the loud laughter, but the man did not bother to give him a glance. Sudhanshu wondered if the speaker's British accent distracted him, as he didn't get much out of the seminar. At lunch break, Sudhanshu told his two friends that he would have to rush to the office to attend to an emergency; he never returned.

Dissecting Sudhanshu Aggarwal

Sudhanshu Aggarwal had paid good money to attend the seminar, and no sooner had he settled down to listen to the speaker his mind began to wander away from the seminar. Let's look at Sudhanshu when he was a toddler. According to Sudhanshu, his mother told him that he was a typical boy – naughty and spoiled. He would flit and fly, wanting to do everything in a jiffy. He was buoyant, exuberant, and he was everywhere. His nursery teachers were pleased with Sudhanshu because he was a happy-go-lucky chap. When asked to relate a story, his imagination would get the better of him and he would make up bizarre tales as he went along. According to Sudhanshu, some of his teachers adored him. But when he entered Class II, cracks began to show in his general aptitude. Sundhanshu remembered his mother complain that after a run of great teachers, the Class II teacher was the first teacher who was not good to Sudhanshu. She was very strict, and she always got after Sushanshu to study, study, and study. Thereafter, subsequent teachers would complain that Sudhanshu disturbed the class with his antics; Sudhanshu never copied homework-to-do from the blackboard. According to his teachers, Sudhanshu had potential but was restless, distracted and academically lazy. He would go off at a tangent – keeping his mind busy with innumerable plots and plans. Sudhanshu believed that he was a fast thinker, while his teachers were slow talkers. By the time Sudhanshu left college and began working, Sudhanshu's brain, which functioned on 'automatic drive,' habitually transported him on another plane while his superiors, colleagues or subordinates talked 'shop policy.'

Dissecting Ehsaas Pandey

As all adults do, Ehsaas Pandey too, functioned on 'automatic drive.' Pandey was keyed in on the speaker and gave him her best shot at listening and registering all that he said. When she was in school and college, she paid attention and listened to her teachers. She was also polite, helpful and altruistic. If someone needed help, she offered her assistance. Cruising on automatic drive at the seminar, she tried to help Sudhanshu by relating the funny incident, but then she missed out on what the speaker was saying and so immediately reverted her attention to the speaker.

Dissecting Shivang Misra

Functioning on 'auto drive', Misra did what he always did from his childhood days. As a student, he listened to his teachers and took down notes. Over the years, Misra developed the art of listening and writing points simultaneously. His brain would quickly filter the husk from the grain, and he would rapidly make notes of important points. It didn't bother him if his classmates fooled around or bugged the teacher; he remained single-minded and focused on the subject. Whatever others did, it didn't bother Misra. He wouldn't allow himself to be distracted. He was intently listening, filtering and making notes of all that he thought was important. His mind was completely tuned in to the speaker. Interestingly, Misra never heard Sudhanshu's question during the seminar.

By the time we are twenty-five, we begin to function on automatic drive. It means, all the data that is stored in the brain from the foetal stage till adulthood, becomes the individual's life-script, which will govern his actions as an adult. As kids, if our emotional brain blocked the aural receptors and we stopped listening to our parents, teachers or instructors, we would find ourselves in the same predicament as Sudhanshu; our brain gets cluttered with stray thoughts instead of absorbing the ideas expressed by the speaker. On the other hand, if we habitually took down notes in class, as we were expected to and listened to our teachers, we could also, like Misra, develop twin skills – listening to the lecture and at the same time jotting notes, which most people find extremely difficult.

Ways to Overcome Distractions

Can restless and distracted individuals (children and adults) re-write their life scripts and learn to pay attention? Yes, they can, provided they can be shown how to do it. I personally believe that the cure lies in the cause, and problems can be cured if we understand the cause. In this case, I attribute restlessness as the cause for distraction. If you are among those who get easily distracted, look for the following signs.

(a) *Physical Restlessness*

Are you fidgety? Do you preen yourself, like re-arrange your hair or clothing, rub body parts, chew fingernails, drum your fingers, doodle, shake your legs or shift positions while sitting? How does this cause distractions, you may ask? Partho Banerjee while listening to a lecture kept moving his legs from time to time. At times he pulled them back and at times he stretched them. "Isn't that normal?" you may ask. "After all, you can't sit like statues through a lecture." Of course, it's normal to move your legs like Partho Banerjee; especially because he was experiencing pain in his feet as his shoelaces were tied a notch too tight. Since his brain re-directed his attention to his aching feet, he wasn't paying attention to the lecture. Banerjee heard the teacher, but wasn't listening to the lecture; he was listening to the cry of his feet. Similarly, when we re-arrange our hair or clothing, chew fingernails, or drum fingers and shake our legs while someone is talking to us, we stop listening, partially or completely, may be even temporarily, and our focus shifts from the talking to concentrate on ourselves.

(b) *Mental Restlessness*

In this instance, you cleverly mask your behaviour as you fake attention. While the teacher is delivering the lecture, your mind is miles away plotting, planning, scheming, or day dreaming all the while, as you sit still and your eyes are fixed, as though in rapt attention, on the teacher. Your aural receptors shut down, and you don't hear a word of what the teacher says, let alone listen to the lecture. Is there hope for such pretenders, you may ask? Yes, you can stimulate your mind to listen if you want to. A good starting point to train your mind to listen would be to change your seat. Sit in the 'listening zone' which could be the area near or around the teacher's desk. Those who sit near the doorway, sit in the 'exit zone.' Their minds are usually outside the classroom than inside. If you sit in the middle rows of desks, then it is obvious you chose to sit in the 'hearing zone.' Hence, it's important to move to the 'listening zone,' – the first three rows. Next, tune in to listen to the teacher from the first word itself. Get ready to write notes relating only to important points. If you attempt to write every spoken word, you'll soon end up frustrated as you'll miss out listening to the rest of the sentence, let alone the complete lecture.

(c) Interrupting & Interjecting

When the teacher talks, don't 'obstruct' the flow of ideas from entering your brain cells by raising objections to the points expressed in the lecture. Wait till the teacher completes the paragraph or lecture before you raise your hand to seek permission to speak. Many students create barriers while listening, either by mentally disagreeing with the points raised in the lecture or verbally opposing the views expressed, even before the teacher has finished the sentence. (Read chapter 3, *If You Listened Better, Wouldn't You Learn More?*). Children develop 'obstructive listening' habits from parents who often disagree, argue and oppose the spouse's views. Also, when children speak, some parents cut them off mid-sentence. They justify those interruptions, saying that they already knew beforehand what the child was going to say or ask. In such a condition, it is only natural that children get into the habit of disagreeing, arguing and opposing their parents. Later, they carry this habit to school and repeat it in class when the teacher teaches. You must realise that the moment you raise your hand to ask a question or when you mentally oppose the speaker's point of view, your aural receptors automatically shut down. Since the inflow of data is shut off by the aural receptors, your intelligent brain is denied access to further information and is unable to process new data. You stop listening to any further information thereafter. In all likelihood, the teacher may continue the lecture and not pay heed to your interruption, or the teacher may ask you to wait till the paragraph/idea/sentence is completed. While you 'wait' your turn, you keep repeating the question or objection in your mind, and your brain stops registering any further inputs from the lecture. To listen smart, you must know the difference between listening to understand and listening to obstruct. When you listen to understand, you raise questions to clarify ideas and concepts. And, when you listen to obstruct, you raise objections to the ideas and concepts.

(d) Avoiding Eye Contact

Children are imitators of parents – their primary educators. Many parents continue to do whatever they are doing when children speak to them. How many parents put down the newspaper, switch off the television or turn down the music, when children talk to them? To teach children the art of listening at home or in class, parents will have to lead by example. Parents will have to look directly into the children's eyes when they speak to them. When you do this, you will want your children, too, to look directly into your eyes when you speak to them. To train children to listen and stay focused on a discussion or lecture, formally or informally, it is a worthwhile endeavour to direct your gaze at them when they talk to you or when you talk to them. Many students avoid eye contact with teachers in class, and this is one of the reasons for physical and mental restlessness. To arrest physical and mental restlessness, the best way is to lock your gaze into the eyes of the speaker. Then let the ears follow the example of the eyes. Thereafter, listening and understanding follows easily.

(e) Nocturnal Disturbances

People with erratic sleep patterns have poor concentration levels. They tend to be irritable, intolerant and display a low-attention span. Many parents are not aware of the importance of inculcating healthy sleep habits in children. Close to bedtime, some children are fed chocolates, ice creams, custards and other sweet foods that stimulate the brain and keep them awake. Parents also give children a glass of milk or other liquids, before going to bed or during the night. Drinking liquids before bedtime and thereafter, puts pressure on the urinary bladder, making the children wake up at night to visit the washroom. Parents should make it a point to ensure that children are not exposed to nocturnal disturbances of any kind. Children should get twelve to eight hours of sleep every night (without napping in the daytime). Parents should ensure an environment where children sleep without interruption every night at fixed hours, say from 8.00 p.m. to 8.00 a.m. for infants and toddlers and 10.00 p.m. to 6.00 a.m. for pre-teens and teens. When children sleep fitfully and uninterruptedly each night, you can be assured they will wake up refreshed and stay focused through the day. Sleep is a great energiser for all of us, including children.

Points to Remember

1. When you interrupt someone, you literally stop listening, as the brain absorbs itself with objections to contradict the speaker.
2. Children learn 'interruption drills' at home at an early age. The technique later gets fine-tuned in class and socially. As grown-ups, they are on 'auto-mode' when they obstruct listening through verbal interruptions.
3. To overcome distractions, control your thoughts from drifting to other issues; and to stop unnecessary bodily movements, sit in the 'listening zone' area. Avoid creating mental barriers by disagreeing with the speaker, even before the speaker has finished speaking.
4. Do not multi-task when speaking to children. Look them in the eye when you talk to them so that they learn to return your gaze when listening and talking to you.
5. Ensure a comfortable environment to improve sleep quality which will increase attention span and concentration.

3

If You Listened Better, Wouldn't You Learn More?

Salient Features

"You never listen," parents scold their children. Who will teach children how to listen? Students spend a huge chunk of their lives in classrooms engaged in 'communication' with teachers, classmates, friends and foes – without training. Students need to know the basic tools of communication, because lectures are not only heard but they also have to be understood and evaluated simultaneously. Basic speaking and listening styles have their origin in families at an early age. This chapter shows how parents can set good examples as role models of effective communication within the family. Since listening is not taught formally, parents may have to train themselves to speak in short sentences and to the point; to use polite expressions and speak in soft tones; and to listen attentively and single-mindedly. If parents find it difficult to learn and adopt new methods to communicate effectively, then how can they expect to inspire and teach children to speak effectively and listen efficiently?

Isn't it ironical that business houses expose their executives to refresher programmes on Effective Communication Skills, while students who sit in classrooms, day-after-day, for many, many years, continuously listening to lectures are never taught even the most elementary lessons on effective communication? 'Listening' is not a school subject like reading and writing. Listening is taken for granted. "Open your ears and listen," we were told as students. Obviously, there is a lot more to listening than merely 'open your ears and listen.' Listening is not simply hearing. Listening has to do with thinking about what is heard, understanding what is heard, and evaluating what is heard.

Understanding the Tools of Communication

In technical jargon, effective communication consists of a transmitter and a receiver which is combined into a single package controlled by a computer. Your brain is the computer which receives multiple inputs and transmits in three mediums – verbal, non-verbal and writing. As a 'single package,' you spend approximately half the time as a transmitter sending out messages and the other half of the time you spend as a receiver receiving messages. If, as a receiver, you mentally switch off or allow yourself to surf channels while someone else is transmitting, you suffer information loss. Similarly, if as a transmitter you permit your narrative to become disorganised, unconvincing or repetitive, you encourage frequency drift. As long as you transmit clearly, efficiently and persuasively, the person receiving the message keeps his receiver switch 'on' to your transmitting frequency. Such conditions expedite information transference, or 'effective communication.'

Communication is a two-way street. You are the speaker and the listener. As a communicator, man is lazy and inefficient. He is equipped with a highly sophisticated communication system, yet consistently fails to use it properly. Through the ages, man has struggled to listen efficiently and to speak effectively. Perhaps the old foundation of education, which necessarily was based on reading and writing, has been replaced with new foundations based on speaking and listening. Education must now include training in speaking and listening along with reading and writing. This training must prepare future citizens to live in a society where spoken communication is more influential than written communication.

Listen with Eyes and Ears

Do you hear better or see better? Are the ears more dominant than the eyes or is it the other way around? While some say they see better than they hear, there are others who say, they hear better than they see. Your emotional brain has charge of the remote control. The emotional brain determines which sense organ filters what information to the intelligent brain. The emotional brain can dull the visual receptors and excite the aural receptors and *vice versa*; this 'doctored' data is then sent to the intelligent (neo cortex) brain for processing. Is it possible to 'see' what we hear? I once heard a child scold his mother in a restaurant, "Mamma, listen to me with your eyes and ears." That loud plea from a six-year old to his mother not only made her put down the menu-card she was scrutinising, but it also summed up a vital lesson on effective listening. It doesn't matter whether it is to do with personal conversation or listen to the teacher in school, we have to train ourselves and our children to listen effectively. Time and again, we will have to remember to remind ourselves not to forget, to remember to listen with our eyes, ears and all our senses in order to listen efficiently.

Being a Good Communicator

It takes two to tango, they say. To nurture the habit of good listening skills in your child, you have to be a good communicator. The first cardinal rule to train children to be good listeners is to ensure that they never 'turn a deaf ear' to what you say. Children who often turn a deaf ear to what parents say, usually see through the contradictions of their parents actions. Before you train your child to be a good listener, you have to train yourself to be a good communicator. As a good communicator, you should always:
a) Speak with clarity and to the point (speak articulately in short, crisp sentences, not paragraphs);
b) Maintain eye-contact with the child when speaking;
c) Switch off the computer, *ipod*, television, radio before you speak;

d) Put aside the newspaper, magazine, book before speaking;
e) Speak softly; never shout or raise your voice;
f) Never speak through closed doors, bathroom doors or bedroom doors;
g) Use a soft, polite tone of voice;
h) Constantly applaud (praise) positive responses (do not take good behaviour for granted; recognition of good behaviour generates more acts of good behaviour);
i) Profusely use expressions like, 'please, thank you, love you or excuse me;'
j) Make the child feel important; feed her self-esteem;
k) Make corrections in private, praise in public.

The second cardinal rule to train children to be good listeners is to ensure that no one – neither your spouse nor any one – contradicts (obstructs) your commands. If, for some reason you denied your child access to, say, the *ipod* for the day, then all the members of the family should also respect that command and not override it. When grown-ups contradict each other over parenting issues, they inadvertently nurture children who habitually throw tantrums. Tantrums are expressed in many forms, depending on your responses. Some children throw themselves on the floor to hurt themselves or embarrass you in public. Others cry, scream, screech, howl, sulk or sob. In extreme cases of frustration, you may have seen kids who punch, pinch, spit, hit, pull hair, clothing, use expletives or throw and break objects around them. All such acts support obstructive listening habits. Obviously, their hostile communication mode blocks their aural receptors and they stop listening to you.

Be a Good Role Model

Being skilled in listening is, in a sense, more important than being skilled in speaking. An average student spends about fifty to seventy-five percent time in the classroom listening. Surely, listening requires training in techniques. The best way to teach children good listening skills is to be a good role model yourself. Parents and teachers can model good listening behaviour for their students and advise them on ways to listen as an active learner. Pick out highlights of a conversation or paragraph and ask relevant questions. Good listening habits get reinforced when parents lock their eyes with their child's, put down the book, magazine or newspaper they are reading, switch off the radio or turn off the television to make sure that the listener is not distracted by outside interference.

The following guidelines will help you to spruce up your transmitter and receiver skills as an effective role model:

Be interested and attentive. Children can tell whether they have their parent's interest and attention by the way the parent replies or does not reply. Look your child in the eye if you want to show that you really are with the child.

Listen to non-verbal messages. Many messages your children send are communicated non-verbally. As you listen to what they say, listen to their tone of voice and watch their facial expressions, their posture, their energy level or changes in their behaviour patterns. You can always tell more from the way a child says something than from what is said.

Encourage talking. Some children need to be coaxed to start talking. They need time to open up to conversation. Children are more likely to share their ideas and feelings, when others think they are important and give them time to open up.

Listen patiently. Grown-ups think faster than they speak. With limited vocabulary and experience in talking, children often take longer than adults to find the right word. Listen as though you have plenty of time.

Listen, don't interrupt. Avoid cutting children off before they have finished speaking. It is easy to form an opinion or reject children's views before they finish what they have to say. At times, it may be difficult to listen respectfully and not correct their misconceptions, but respect their right to have opinions and express them.

Ways to Improve Effective Communication

The family is the training ground for learning effective communication skills since it is not a school subject. Parents have to teach themselves techniques to communicate effectively so that they generate an easy flow of conversation in the family, especially with their pre-teens and teens. The following five points will help you to break the ice and chill out with your pre-teens and teens.

1) Enter your child's world. Learn to 'hang out' with your children at least twice a week. Use their idiom and imagery when you talk to them. Listen to their music; ask them to teach you a new game; get introduced to their school friends. When you enter their world, don't censure, don't object, don't give your opinion; just go with the flow. This may be difficult for many parents at the beginning; after a while, with some sincere effort, it gets easier.

2) Show you're sincere. Talk one-to-one with your children and show them that you are interested in who their friends are, in what they like doing, what they feel and what they think, while you maintain eye contact all the time. If you regularly ask them for opinions and ideas, they will become comfortable in expressing their ideas to you.

3) Avoid talking in monosyllables. Speak in sentences, not in monosyllables. Your questions and answers should extend the line of conversation, not cut it off. Avoid dead-end questions. Questions that require a 'yes,' 'no' or 'right' answers lead the conversation to a dead-end. Ask your children to describe, explain or share ideas. This will extend the line of conversation.

4) Involve children in housekeeping. Instead of telling them, "Keep your room clean and tidy," share your thoughts on a larger scale. You can get started by allocating minor household chores. The next step is to show them how the job should be done and where to keep the cleaning equipment so that whoever wants to use it again will easily find it. Applaud, or praise when the chore is completed. The benefits of housekeeping are manifold; the most important is having pride for one's home. You must involve children in housekeeping decisions. For instance, when you paint your home, or get new curtains, upholstery, towels, bed linen, table napkins or re-arrange furniture, ask for their opinion; ask questions.

5) Never force children to communicate. Never impose a 'chat session' with children. Watch them closely for signs when it's time to end the conversation. When children stare into space, get busy with some activity, give silly answers or ask you to repeat several of your comments, it is probably time to stop the conversation. If you rebuke them, patronise them or lecture them, you are missing the purpose of the entire exercise.

6) Reflect feelings. A good listener is a keen observer of moods. Inculcate the ability, not only to step into the shoes of your child, but also get inside his skin. Once inside his skin, understanding his thoughts and feelings becomes easier. As a parent, try to reflect your child's feelings by verbalising them. For instance, you might mirror your child's feelings by saying, "It sounds as if you are angry at me." Re-stating or re-phrasing what children have said is useful when they are experiencing powerful emotions that they may not be fully aware of.

7) Re-stating and re-phrasing words. As you listen, re-state and re-phrase your child's feelings in your own words, your enriched vocabulary will help children express themselves accurately and clearly and give them a deeper understanding of words, idioms and inner thoughts. When you speak to them do not mix languages. If you speak to them in English, do not mix English with Bengali, Hindi, Tamil, etc., and *vice versa*. Keep your language chaste at all times, and you will be pleased to hear them speak well after a while.

Parents play an essential role in building children's communication skills. Sons pick up speech mannerisms from their fathers, and daughters pick up speech mannerisms from their mothers. Children have a deeper contact with their parents than with outside adults. Parents set a powerful example of good or bad communication. In urban India, children from well-to-do families spend more time with maids and nannies than with parents. Often their speech mannerisms and listening skills replicate those of the maids or nannies. The greatest audience children can have is an adult who is important to them and interested in them. Is it you or is it the nanny? Parents who listen to children with interest, attention and patience, set good examples of effective speaking and efficient listening.

Points to Remember

1. Listening is an art which has to be learnt. Listening involves *thinking, understanding*, and *evaluating* all that is heard.
2. As a good communicator, you are the transmitter who has to transmit messages clearly and efficiently so that receivers stay locked on to the transmitting 'frequency.'
3. Parents are role models for good or bad communication because children speak and listen the way they are spoken to and listened to.
4. Bonding is absolutely important to help them open up to you. Listen when they talk about their aspirations, dreams and ambitions. Avoid talking in monosyllables. Be sensitive not only to what they say but also to body language cues. Re-phrase in your own words the child's feelings.
5. When you listen to children with interest, attention and patience, you set a good example for them to copy.

4

Why Throttle Untapped Potential?

Salient Features
Many students put a lot of sincere effort into studying. In spite of the hard work, they still earn average to poor grades. The thought of failure frustrates them to the point where, at times, they stop studying altogether. In school they are treated as outcasts; at home they are called good-for-nothings. It is time for parents to have the right perspective of what schools offer as education. Since 1983, Dr Howard Gardner has shown the world that the human brain has eight intelligences. In spite of this 'discovery,' the school curriculum arbitrarily continues to teach and test students at two levels of intelligences, while throttling the untapped potential of students in other fields. Parents believe in the system of education, and rightly so, because education alone ensures great jobs and a secure future. But, the education system has failed to explore the full extent of talents and potential of the students it serves. Hence parents ought to prioritise. Is it worth the while to stress kids and force them to study subjects that are difficult, tedious and strenuous? Or is it worth the while to explore children's talents and potential, along with schooling, laying emphasis on the holistic development of kids, rather than creating academic wizards?

Vikram and his wife Aanya, complained about their nine-year-old Vanshika who hated her teachers, her books and most of her classmates. Each term, she would barely scrape through her exams. Aanya was at her wits end, exhausted and drained at the end of each day, trying to outwit Vanshika, who had mastered the art of keeping her mother guessing while she did what she enjoyed doing most – staying one step ahead of her mom. The little nine-year-old, according to Aanya, glibly told lies, was cheeky, manipulative, threw tantrums, stole money, and had no recollection where she'd 'forgot' her textbooks, copybooks, notebooks, pencils, pens and anything that was related to schooling.

Vikram and Aanya assured me that they had tried everything to help Vanshika; Aanya admitted that she hit her out of frustration – but the "little monster was shameless." They felt convinced that boarding school was the only place which would straighten her out. I disagreed.

For parents like Vikram and Aanya, schooling is nerve-racking; especially when children struggle to cope with studies. The parents desperately look for ways and means, either through private tuition, coaching classes or boarding schools, to help children make the grade and hopefully to turn a new leaf. When that fails, they silently cry themselves at nights, praying that their child would somehow turn a new leaf and do well in studies like 'normal' kids do. They soon lose faith in themselves, as parents, when their prayers go unanswered.

Schooling isn't the 'end-all' of student life

It is common knowledge that schools play a very important role in a child's life. Bereft of schooling, children would remain illiterate, unskilled and jobless. Without undermining the importance of schooling in a child's formative years, I would like to caution you that in our zeal to make children literate, skilled and job-oriented, we mustn't treat academics as the one and only goal of interest in their developmental years. The sooner parents and teachers realise that academics isn't the 'end-all' of a child's life on this planet – that there is more to life than academics – only then will parents and teachers realise the importance of helping children to make each day count. Why do we automatically conclude that all school-going children should excel in studies? Haven't we heard academicians tell us that humans have eight levels of intelligences? May be more? Did you know that schools do not evaluate children on the eight levels of intelligences? Did you know that out of the two or three levels of intelligences which the school evaluates your child on, it could be that those are the very levels your child is not interested in? The more you hammer at the child to master academics, the more you damage her self-esteem, her trust and her belief in you as nurturing parents. What is more important to you – nurturing happiness in children or nurturing bookworms? What good is a Ph.D. gold medallist who ends up being a lousy individual – a cranky crab who is difficult to live with?

To find out Vanshika's untapped potential, I asked her parents what their child enjoyed doing. With some hesitation (as they began to think hard) they enumerated Vanshika's talents. She loved singing, music, dancing and drawing. Vanshika also played tennis at the local club. She was kind to animals in distress and got emotionally disturbed when she saw urchin kids beg at street corners. Indeed, what a wealth of talent this child was endowed with. Unfortunately, Vanshika's school will never award her recognition for any of these talents. Parents and teachers must ask themselves, is the anxiety and hostility worth it? When will it dawn on us that our children are gifted with so much potential? When will parents and teachers pull down the shroud of academics from their children's shoulders and uncover their untapped potential?

Most parents look upon academics as a long-term investment, where children pick up skills to last a lifetime. That's a fallacy. The period of schooling is nothing but a chunk of a child's time, from the toddler-age till the child is sixteen years old, which shelters him from earning a wage. He is subjected to an environment where he is kept occupied till he grows up to take on responsibilities. Unfortunately, schooling has hardly turned a child around to be 'man enough to take on responsibilities.' If there are any such cases in the affirmative then you may credit that 'development' to effective parenting.

Do you think Vanshika, and many more like her who struggle with academics, will pick up study skills to last a lifetime? Or, do you think academics will teach Vanshika to be responsible and accountable for her actions as an adult? For millions of families, schooling is a huge drain as an investment – an investment that rarely benefits children *en masse*. Schooling is short-term; it will last till the time the student is sixteen years old. After writing the final Board exams, it will all be over for Vanshika and her classmates; they will be on their own thereafter. And, then what, you may ask? Are they ready to take on life's challenges?

It is unfortunate to note that parents, in their zeal to ram academics down the throats of their children, erode the glue that binds children to them – the glue of happiness. Time and again we see children who are nurtured on a daily diet of 'pressure' to cram, end up hitting back at parents with the only weapon they are familiar with – defiance, hostility and indifference.

I have counselled many students who sacrificed their childhood, every hobby, every pleasurable moment at the altar of academics. They slogged untiringly at academics so that they could pursue higher studies in the finest colleges of their choice. They ate, drank, slept and breathed the air of academics. Their lives alternated between school and tutors for three hundred and sixty-five days of the year, without a break, for a number of years. Then, in the final Board exams, they scored an aggregate of ninety percent to ninety-five percent. Instead of being elated, they felt deflated, depressed, dejected and their egos bruised. What was the reason for sadness, you would ask? The reason was they were unable to get admission to the finest colleges of their choice and pursue the subjects of their choice. They had to settle for a compromise. Either accept the college of their choice minus the subjects of their choice or pursue the subjects of their choice in the next best college. In one stroke, their entire world had collapsed. They were high on IQ but pretty low on EQ (emotional quotient) and SQ (social quotient).

If such fate awaits students scoring ninety-five percent – the *crème de la crème* of academics, then what is to become of the several lakh students who score sixty percent and below? Parents and teachers should be more considerate of students who are unable to score high in school tests and exams. They have vast reservoirs of social, emotional, kinaesthetic, musical and other untapped potential. Why throttle that untapped potential? What good is a Ph.D. scholar who ends up being a lousy human being? A lousy human being makes life miserable for his family, his spouse, his friends and everybody around him.

Strike the Right Balance

In spite of such a scenario, parents like Vikram and Aanya and a million others, want desperately for their children to succeed in academics. Why? Is it to enter the best colleges? Or, is it because mastering academics is the end-all of a student's life? To achieve those ends, parents single-mindedly get their children to conform to schooling at the cost of denying them opportunities to explore and develop their natural talents. Ironically, those could be the very talents which students may have to rely on in adult life, but which go unrecognised in the schools they study in. Once out of school, what happens? Students leaving school will be bereft of hobbies and interests because the teachers and parents in their zeal to teach them the art of cramming academics throttled those hobbies and interests. Academics are short-term and time bound. Which student has gone back to reading his class notes or old textbooks as a hobby? But a student, who participates in sports, music, dance, drama etc., will nurture many more interests and hobbies provided his parents helped him to sustain those hobbies and interests – in spite of schooling.

Prepare children for a life after school. Give them life skills. Inject in them large doses of happiness. Let them learn to be happy individuals who will make others happy. At the end of each day, parents should ask themselves, "Did we make our kids happy today?" And, "Have we stimulated in them happy thoughts?" When you consciously work to make your kids happy, you will open the floodgates of their hidden potential. Imagine, living life to one's full potential – not theoretically but realistically. Make your children happy individuals and you would have succeeded in giving them the best education to last a lifetime.

Compartments and Labels

It is so easy to label students into categories and place them in compartments – dull ones, bright ones and average kids. We don't realise that we use an ancient yardstick to measure our children's intelligence levels. The yardstick relates to the child's ability to master language and logic. Educators and psychologists label kids who are unable to master reading, writing and math skills, as dullards. (Once, a distraught parent asked me to help her with her "idiot son." Within six months of attending my workshops, the parents began to speak of their son with pride). After labelling students as duffers, do the experts offer professional help, like new learning techniques to stimulate the child's cognitive brain? No, they don't. After labelling kids, the experts and specialists wash their hands off them, as though some duty to humanity was satisfactorily performed and it's business as usual – time to move on to prepare another IQ test!

And what would happen if we didn't label students and put them in compartments? Would the roof fall on our heads? No, it wouldn't. In all probability the experts and specialists, along with parents and teachers, would have no choice but to apply their minds at improving student-learning skills. Many would find new ways at improving their personal skills in order to reach out effectively to students who are slow at comprehending words, numbers or have trouble remembering and recalling. They would apply new techniques and skills to reach out and help the students to learn effectively. In doing so, we as a society would successfully tap other talents and interests that lie dormant in students.

Dr Howard Gardner, professor of Education at Harvard University, developed the theory of Multiple Intelligences (MI) in 1983. The theory propounded that the traditional notion of intelligence, based on IQ testing, was far too limited. He proposed eight different intelligences to account for a broader range of human potential in children and adults, which are employed in a variety of ways and in a variety of settings, including work and educational settings. The following are the eight intelligences:

1) Verbal (Linguistic) Intelligence:
This has to do with the ability to speak, read and write fluently. Specifically, verbal intelligence helps to display a facility with words and languages. Students with verbal intelligence tend to learn best by reading, taking notes and listening to lectures, discussions and debates. They are also skilled at explaining and speaking. Those with verbal intelligence have high verbal memory and recall and an ability to understand and manipulate syntax and structure (Gardner 1993).

2) Mathematical-logical Intelligence:
This has to do with the ability to do mathematical concepts and think logically. Individuals with mathematical-logical intelligence, possess reasoning capabilities, abstract pattern recognition, scientific thinking and investigation, and the ability to perform complex calculations. This intelligence indicates the ability to use and understand numbers and apply reasoning skills to explain relationships and abstractions.

3) Visual-spatial Intelligence:
This type of intelligence deals with the perception of visual and spatial world. Those with visual-spatial intelligence

generally have a very good sense of direction and may also have very good eye-hand co-ordination. They possess the capacity to transform their perceptions into form, colour, space and relationships. (Thomas Armstrong, 1994). They also have the ability to form mental images of concepts and of their personal experiences and to transform these images into personal meaning and applications.

4) Intrapersonal Intelligence:

Those who possess this intelligence are those who are believed to have more self-knowledge and tend to be more introspective, reflective and cognitively and consciously self-aware and prefer to work alone. Their self-awareness makes them capable of understanding their own emotions, goals and motivations. They learn best when allowed to concentrate on the subjects by themselves. (Gardner, 1999). There is often a high level of perfectionism associated with this intelligence, and they tend to be aware of their personal strengths and weaknesses.

5) Interpersonal Intelligence:

People in this category are likely to indulge in and foster successful relationships and are characterised by their sensitivity to others' moods, feelings, temperaments and motivations and their ability to co-operate, in order to work as a group. They can communicate effectively and empathise easily with others when working in groups and may be either leaders or followers. (Gardner, 1993). They communicate effectively and possess the ability to persuade others; they typically learn best by working with others and often enjoy discussion and debate. They are attentive to non-verbal factors such as facial expressions, bodily gestures and voice.

6) Body-kinaesthetic Intelligence:

This intelligence helps people to acquire the expertise in using the whole body to express ideas and feelings and the ability to building and making things. They often learn best by physically doing something, rather than reading or hearing about it. Those with body-kinaesthetic intelligence seem to remember things through their body, rather than through words (verbal memory) or images (visual memory). They benefit from working with others in experiential situations, which allows for non-verbal implications rather than verbal communication. (Gardner, 1999).

7) Musical Intelligence:
People who possess this intelligence, use rhythms, music and sounds to illustrate and communicate creative thinking. Those who have a high level of musical-rhythmic intelligence display greater sensitivity to sounds, rhythms, and music. Since there is a strong aural component to this intelligence, those who are strongest in it may learn best via lecture and oral stimulation. In addition, they will often use rhythms to learn and memorise information and may work best with soft background music playing. (Gardner, 1993).

8) Naturalistic Intelligence:
This intelligence pertains to the ability to understand and be in tune with nature. It is believed that this is the newest of the intelligences and concerns people who have the capacity to recognise and make distinctions between the natural and the artificial dimensions of things in the world. Those who possess this intelligence have greater sensitivity to nature and their place within it, the ability to nurture and grow things and have greater ease in caring for, taming and interacting with animals. They are also good at recognising and classifying different species. (Gardner, 1999).

Can You Teach an Old Dog New Tricks?
In the age of information technology where learning knows no barriers, the very temples of learning raise barriers by denying recognition of the existence of multiple intelligences as proposed by Dr Howard Gardner. In the age of information technology, it is an aberration for schools to rely on age-old traditional subjects, which severely limits the imparting of

holistic education and learning. Unfortunately, students who are gifted with intelligences other than logic and language, continue to experience pressure, stress and failure in coping with schooling. To incorporate the eight intelligences into the school curriculum would call for a brand new teaching and learning format. The old format will have to be overhauled, in parts or in whole, and that may take decades. In the meanwhile, we should at least stop punishing students for the failure of the system.

Can students be protected from the indignity of failure, caused by the failure of the education system to re-frame its curriculum to absorb other intelligences which would account for a broader range of human potential? (Read chapter 8, *Study Smart and Get to a Flying Start*). The PTA bodies in schools could play a proactive role in protecting students from failure, stress and pressure. We need to bring immediate relief to students. We don't need a revolution to re-frame the curriculum. We need to give students better and effective tools to cope with the curriculum. Schools need to bring in the 'soft skills' gurus. The 'soft skills' experts will utilise modern research and apply its findings to teach students modern techniques (pertaining to social, spiritual, mental, emotional, intellectual and physical aspects) in coping with the curriculum. The 'soft skills' experts will also train teachers in understanding the diversity of intelligences of students in the class, and adopt varied skills to reach out to them within the framework of the curriculum. Parents, too, can update their parenting techniques from the 'soft skills' gurus so that home and school will work in unison in promoting a stress-free learning environment. This 'revolution' will be far more effective in transforming the lives of millions of students by giving free expression to the potential lying either untapped or throttled.

Points to Remember

1. When children are unable to cope with the pressure of academics, they display inappropriate behaviour.
2. Academic learning is important but it should not be treated as the 'end-all' of a child's life. There is a lot more to holistic development than academics.
3. Parents must strike the right balance between academics and nurturing hobbies and interests in children.
4. Schools must explore all the eight intelligences as researched by Dr Howard Gardner, so that the students' potential is not throttled.
5. Teaching students, parents and teachers 'soft skills' by professionals will soften the burden of academics. Through 'soft skills' they will explore alternate methods to guide students to cope with studies, and parents and teachers to cope with the pressures of life.

5

Don't Get Rundown by Stress

Salient Features

Stress can destroy lives. Mental health problems traumatise students. The school environment can be a very hostile arena where battles rage on different fronts. 'Mind Wars' like high expectations of parents, peer pressure and popularity contests are fought alongside 'Performance Wars,' where students suffer from sleep deprivation due to academic overload, tight schedules, and performance expectations from teachers. Simultaneously, 'Behaviour Wars' which are release valves for tension and pressure, keep stress simmering like a pressure cooker for years. To sensitise yourself to stress, you need to identify signs of its manifestations: physiological, emotional, physical, psychological and behavioural. You can beat stress if you employ appropriate stress busters. Avoid procrastination, set priorities, be positive, switch off objects of distractions, develop good support systems, follow recreation rules and quit cramming.

Stress Can Destroy Lives

Mukesh Chakraborty was nine years old and ailing. His mother, Shalini, looked haggard and spoke in a tired voice when she came to consult me. She was nursing a one-year-old infant, also. For approximately seven months, Mukesh's life revolved around clinics, nursing homes and hospitals, meeting paediatricians, endocrinologists and other specialists. According to Shalini, there was not a single doctor in town whom she had not heard of, met or consulted; but, Mukesh was sick, weak and cranky with no appetite whatsoever. With lots of difficulty, the mother would coax a few teaspoons of water into the child. The foods he ate triggered the irritable bowel syndrome, which led to instant dysentery. With the immune system battered, the child lived from one viral infection to another. Shalini showed me one of Mukesh's medical files. The blood reports showed 'no infection.' The doctors also certified that the child had no chronic ailments. And yet, the child was ailing – chronically. "Mukesh has a stomach ailment that the doctors are unable to diagnose," said Shalini in despair.

After discussing Mukesh's story for about fifty minutes, Shalini was exhausted and asked for a glass of water. As she sipped the water, I asked why her husband did not accompany her to the meeting. Shalini had to manage the two kids on her own because her husband was going through a rough patch in his business. His business partner had duped him. He was very upset about losing a lot of money and clients. When her cellular phone rang, I asked Shalini to answer the phone. Instead she switched it off. I looked puzzled and asked why she didn't take the call? She said, it was her husband, Subash calling. "Why should I spoil my mood? He'll only yell at me," she said.

I glanced at some of the test reports and asked her what if the reports were right and the doctors' certification was correct? In other words, what if Mukesh had no infection and he was not chronically or medically ill? She protested as she pointed to the medical files on my table. I asked Shalini if she had relatives outside Delhi. She said she had a brother in Pune who regularly pleaded to her to come over. I seized the opportunity and told her to pack her bags and take the two kids to Pune for a month. The change would heal Mukesh and he would return to Delhi in good health. Her instant reaction was, "My husband would kill me if I went without him." Strong words from a woman worn down from bringing up two kids. Strong words from a woman about her husband who was duped by a business partner and was working very hard to salvage his business. I asked Shalini if she wanted to talk about the fear of being killed. Silence. For a long time she stared at me. Slowly she broke down, first the tears, then the sobs and finally the loud howls of pain, anguish and despair. Her mind, body and soul, wracked with convulsive sobs as she re-lived memories of eleven years of marriage. And, through her tears, for the first time, she began to see her son grow up through the prism of stress.

Mukesh was afraid of his father. He was witness to many blows that landed on his mother's head, face, shoulders, chest, everywhere. According to Shalini, it didn't take a moment for a simple question or sentence to turn into an argument, and for an argument to turn into ugly blows. When Mukesh cried, each time he saw his mother being hit, Subash would shout abuses, ordering her to get the child to shut up. Trembling, Mukesh would urinate in fear and that would bring on another round of abuses, accusing her of failing to give the child healthy habits. One horror story led to another.

Through the catharsis of tears, Shalini began to see Mukesh's ailments in a new light. Mukesh's ailments were psychosomatic. They were stress related. I pushed harder for her to take the trip to Pune. It would heal Mukesh, though temporarily. Once he returned to Delhi, under the stressful stimuli of the father, Mukesh would wither and live like a vegetable. If Mukesh were to live a normal, healthy life, the father would need to consider psychological help. He would need to learn to control and manage anger, change his attitude and learn not to blame his wife and children for his business failures. Shalini was certain Subash would never consult a counsellor.

Shalini was also nursing a one-year-old infant. She was not sleeping the nights because she woke up intermittently to feed the baby. With all the tension, pressure and stress inside her, her brain produced large volumes of cortisol, the stress chemical. (See chapter 6, *Positive Juices Stimulate the Brain*). This stress chemical flowed in her bloodstream. The infant was being fed cortisol through the mother's milk.

According to Shalini, the baby was so high strung, cranky and irritable. Looking after two kids, being sleep deprived, living in fear with a hot-tempered and violent husband, Shalini was filled with anxiety with the thought that if she died her children would be abandoned.

If Shalini and Subash did not take immediate steps to remedy the stress in the family, the one-year-old infant would soon imbibe the elder child's psychosomatic symptoms and magnify those symptoms. For Shalini, the time to take a stand was imminent. First, she would have to visit Pune (or any other place away from her husband) with her two kids to see if their health improved in a stress-free environment. Second, while in Pune, she would have to do some very serious thinking about the future – how she and her kids could find peace, harmony and happiness to live stress-free lives. Indeed, a difficult decision, especially for a woman so completely dependent on her husband.

Why students live with stress?

With or without family squabbles, the teenage years can be one of the most stressful periods of childhood. Studies show that students learn less and retain less when they are under stress. Mental health problems among students are widespread, due to high stress levels. Academic pressures, heavy work loads, busy schedules, tests and exams, peer pressure, sleep deprivation, high expectations of parents, performance expectations by teachers and the desire to be popular are factors that generate stress. Stress can cause students to develop learning deficiencies, skip classes, miss assignments, underachieve or drop out altogether. Many students silently suffer from high stress levels for years without identifying it or knowing that it can be corrected.

Most mental health problems can be overcome as shown in the chapters of this book. The trigger points for stress, tension and pressure could be strict or unsupervised parenting style, academics, school campus and poor self-image.

Parenting Style: Dominating, critical, hostile parents who mix strict discipline with inflexible rules; or the other way around, liberal rules without supervision usually generate stressful relationships in families.

Academics: Without putting in place an effective 'support system' for students to succeed in academics and/or having high expectations for outstanding performance in exams can break them down. On the other hand, lack of competency in completing academic tasks on the part of students, usually trigger psychological problems.

School Campus: Competing to be the most popular student could turn on a lot of pressure. Also, students with mediocre capabilities who think highly of themselves, put on superior airs, bully classmates and treat friends condescendingly, generate campus stress.

Poor Self-image: Students who are shy, timid and self-effacing, do poorly because they think poorly of themselves and underperform. For instance, they entertain thoughts like, "I'm good for nothing," and they feel, "others are cleverer than I am." Their performance takes a dip because they devalue themselves and think they are incompetent and lacking in intelligence. Usually parents who are critical, demanding, insulting or perfectionists nurture children with poor self-image.

Students displaying stress, tension and pressure, need immediate help so that negative thinking, feelings and behaviour can be corrected and channelled appropriately. When these symptoms go unnoticed and stress builds up to unhealthy levels, students begin to indulge in tobacco, alcohol, drugs, casual sex, pornography and 'comfort' foods for release and relaxation.

How to identify stress signals?

Parents have to be sensitive to identify stress signals in their children. In most cases, reactions and overreactions in families that mostly end up in squabbles generate more stress than relief. When you refuse to get drawn into squabbles, you are better equipped to identify stressful behaviour. You can objectively identify stress symptoms that can be categorised into physiological, physical, mental, emotional and behavioural signals. These are manifested as follows:

1. Physiological Manifestation
You will notice many changes in your child's physiology which indicate stress. Physiological manifestation includes, rapid breathing, increased heartbeat, tense muscles, increased sweating, dry mouth, urge to empty bladder, diarrhoea, feeling of nausea, 'butterflies in stomach' and cold hands and feet.

2. Physical Manifestation
Physical manifestation of stress are frequent colds, change in appetite, complaints of aches and pains, feeling tired, and the worsening of back pain, asthma, digestive problems, headaches and skin eruptions. They spend hours online or over the telephone or listen to music in excess.

3. Emotional Manifestation
Emotional manifestation of stress shows that students are unable to focus and concentrate, have low-attention span, get easily distracted, are overanxious, cry easily, want to be left alone, are frustrated and short tempered. Since stress damages their positive frame of mind, they lose confidence in their abilities; they are unable to think clearly, are confused and make wrong decisions.

4. Mental Manifestation
Stress affects moods. Students under stress may manifest the following mood changes – depression, frustration, hostility, loneliness, helplessness, impatience, irritability and restlessness.

5. Behaviour Manifestation (psychologically)
When students are under stress, they talk too loud or too fast, fiddle with objects, twitch nose, bite nails, grind teeth, drum fingers and become irritable, defensive, critical,

aggressive and irrational, overreact emotionally and become unreasonably negative. They neglect their personal appearance, want to be left alone, talk negatively about school, teachers, friends, family or self. Being unable to concentrate they become more forgetful and make more mistakes.

6. Behaviour Manifestation (physically)

Sometimes stress can be so overwhelming that it results in depression or other serious problems. If you notice any of the following signs of chronic stress in your teenager, get professional help right away – intense or sustained feelings of sadness or depression, hints at ending life, or talk about life after death, use of alcohol or drugs, uncontrollable behaviour, intense or sustained anger, grades toppling, skipping school, running away and eating disorders.

Stress is not hard to beat

You can beat stress if you don't beat about the bush. Students should get this fact straight. The job of pre-teens and teens is to study. Unfortunately, many students approach studies as though they are doing their parents and teachers a favour. They have to be reminded again and again that, like parents, they too hold a job and that job is to study. Students have to accept responsibility for the manner in which they execute their job. The quicker they get down to the job of studying, knowing that there is nobody else who is going to do it for them, the sooner they will clear a major stress hurdle. Some parents exhibit helplessness when teens revolt or disobey them. Parents ought to know when to be firm and when to be lenient. You cannot be firm in all situations of disobedience and neither can you be lenient in all situations of revolt. There are times when you may have to look the other way and not nag the child. And, there are times when you will have to take a stand and firmly take away certain privileges until the teenager earns it back through good performance. The best way to deal with academic stress is to have good study habits and an effective time management system. In short, students need to learn how to prioritise, organise and execute.

1. Don't Procrastinate

Procrastination is putting off or avoiding doing something that must be done. It is natural to procrastinate occasionally. However, excessive procrastination can result in

(i) guilty feelings (for not doing the task),

(ii) anxiety feelings (since the task remains undone), and

(iii) poor quality work (since the task was hurriedly completed).

All these factors not only breed stress but also interfere with academic and personal success.

2. First Things First

When you sit to study, don't put off important matters because it is difficult. Most students busy themselves during home study attending to subjects of least importance, leaving the tedious stuff for the last moment which may never get done. Take the tough, dreaded bulls head on and while in the ring, soon you will see that you are capable of taking the bulls by their horns and keep them under control. Once you learn techniques on ways to take charge of the tough subjects and accomplish them, stress will gradually fade away.

3. Positive Approach

Remind yourself that you can do almost anything if you put your mind to it. Believe in yourself to give yourself a convincing pep talk from time to time, and get going. (See Chapter 6, *Positive Juices Stimulate the Brain*). Once you are into the task, you will probably find that it is more interesting than you thought it would be and definitely not as difficult as you had feared. You will feel increasingly relieved as you work towards its accomplishment. The satisfaction you will experience on completing the task will act as the stress-buster, and you will begin to take on other tough assignments that earlier seemed intimidating.

4. Banish Electronic Gadgets

There is a time for everything – a time to work seriously, and a time to while away time. While studying, beware of the internet. The 'search engine' can soak up precious time so deviously that you are often unaware of it. How easily a simple online task can end up taking an hour or more! Act smart! Have an action plan before switching on the electronic time guzzler that you call the PC. Devise a strategy and stay with it. Log on to the internet, use it as your slave to serve you (to get what you want), then log off. As for the cell phone, switch it off and leave it in some other room to kill the temptation of reaching for it. The television, radio, ipods, PSP, MP3, DVD and all distracting objects should remain off limits during study time.

5. Positive Support Systems

To succeed, every student needs a good support system. The family always is the first and strongest support system that students depend on. As the first tier of the support system, families have to regulate their schedules for television viewing, outings, chit-chat, entertainment, mealtimes and sleep hours to accommodate the child's timetable. As parents, the finest support system you can give your children is to personally serve them hot breakfast every morning with a 'goodbye' hug before they leave for school. After family, the friends your child hangs out with, forms the second tier of support system. Just like birds of a feather flock together, average students mostly cluster with average friends, the bright students cluster with the bright ones, sports students hang out with other sports enthusiasts, and so on. Parents need to watch out and regulate the second tier of the support system to ensure that friends do not pass on bad habits, distract and waste their time or lure them away from studying.

6. Recreation Rules

The first and second tiers of the support system (parents and friends) and the students need to have a common approach on how and when to recreate. Leisure is best enjoyed after completing assignments or after a hard day's work. If assignments are put aside in favour of recreation, then instead of recreation or relieving stress, the pressure of incomplete assignments mounts and so does stress. Recreation should relax you and should be used to beat stress, not the other way around.

7. Quit Cramming

There is no learning value to cramming. Overnight cramming or committing yourself to marathon study sessions the night before the exams are less productive and the matter is quickly forgotten, at times even before the papers are attempted. Usually when procrastination sets in, cramming follows automatically. To ensure that the fear of exams do not stress you, make a conscious effort to commit yourself to daily home study. It is far more beneficial to study every day, maybe in shorter but more frequent intervals, than to study just before the exams. Daily study has the following advantages:

(i) It keeps information fresh in the mind and drastically cuts down time on re-learning the same matter again and again.

(ii) Revisions will be faster and less tedious as the matter will be familiar and easy to follow.

(iii) Understanding and retention of the matter learnt will stay long after the final exams.

The best outcome of this practice is that students will stop cramming, retain more and control stress.

Turn On the Receptive Mood

Did you know that when you are happy, you not only enjoy what you do but you also learn faster? Research reveals that people are more likely to give a favourable evaluation when they are in a positive frame of mind, and a negative evaluation when they are in a negative frame of mind. Teachers, who begin their classes on a positive note, ignite a receptive mood in students. And, teachers, who begin the class either by scolding students or plunge into the subject straightaway, tune off many students. To open the minds of students, use the receptive route. At home, parents should relax the kids and put them in a happy frame of mind before beginning the study hour. A negative frame of mind makes the study hour loathsome and tedious.

Use Positive Energy to Dispel Stress

When students display stress, it is usually that the environment they live in is stressful. Some parents whirl in their own orbits, without realising that they also have a life outside the career orbit. If children are expected to excel at their jobs without stress, then parents have a responsibility to offer children a healthy support system at home. Unfortunately, without realising it, parents offload office stress at home. The unfortunate children are left with no choice but to adapt and adjust to the stress moods of parents. The stress moods could swing from liberal parenting style, (total indifference to the children's needs), to absolute-control parenting style, (parents rant, rave, scold and beat children for supposedly bad behaviour). In some homes, spouses spend evenings trading verbal and physical abuses. Stress takes its toll on the children whenever parents engage themselves in tiffs and wars, like rival teams competing in a slanging match, destroying the fabric of family joy. Imagine two high-voltage live wires, negative and positive, causing sparks each time they come in contact; a short circuit plunges the whole house into darkness. On the other hand, imagine two high-voltage live wires that reside cosily side by side inside a coated cable. The negative and positive wires, when charged, energise the whole house with light. Why short circuit your homes when you can energise everyone with the power of love and happiness?

Points to Remember

1. Students are silent victims of stress-related diseases.
2. Mental health problems can be corrected provided parents sensitise themselves to how they are manifested.
3. Strict parenting styles, low academic performance, campus stress or poor self-image could drive students to aberrant behaviour – drugs, alcohol, tobacco, unhealthy eating habits and unhealthy sexual curiosity.
4. A positive family support system gives students positive energy to dispel stress.
5. You can pre-empt stress, tension and pressure through the appropriate use of stress busters by improving lifestyle habits.

6

Positive Juices Stimulate the Brain

Salient Features

When students perform poorly, say in maths or science, the first casualty are hobbies and interests. No more fun-stuff. Arrangements are made for extra home study or tutors to fill in the gaps. This is a hasty and misguided step in effective parenting. When students play musical instruments, outdoor games, dramatics, arts and other extra-curricular activities, it gives them a great of deal of happiness; and if they excel in any one of them, it brings them pride and appreciation. By putting a stop to these activities, you shut off the positive juices (cranial fluids) from being produced and released by the brain. Positive fluids, like dopamine, are released when the brain receives happy inputs. Negative fluids, like cortisol, are released when the brain receives stress inputs. It is common knowledge that the power of the brain varies depending on the fluids it receives. You can dramatically increase the power and efficiency of your brain by optimising the positive flow of its cranial fluid. For instance, you may have entered examination halls, at times apprehensively, at times confidently. The times when you were apprehensive would be the toughest exams you took, and the times you were confident would be the best exams you took. You can apply these principles of positivity to improve your performance in subjects that are tough and tedious, provided you feed your brain with a balanced diet, regular exercises, sound sleep habits and a positive environment.

We have three brains lodged in our heads – the intelligent brain, which is located in the forehead of the skull; the emotional brain, which is located in the mid-section of the skull; and the oldest brain, the reptilian brain, which is located at the lower back of the head. Much before the time of Socrates, it was accepted that the intelligent brain was superior to the emotional brain because reason was superior to emotions. The origins of intellectual superiority can be traced to the Greeks who taught *didactics* (logic) in schools and universities. The Romans learnt from the Greeks. The Greco-Roman culture spread all over Europe and the British set up schools and universities everywhere they ruled.

Intelligence Linked to Emotions

When students are unable to cope with academics, we automatically conclude that they are lazy in exercising their intelligence or they are preoccupied and distracted with games and hobbies or worse still, they are less intelligent than other students. Whenever students fare poorly in some subjects, teachers often advice parents to curtail entertainment, games, hobbies and other co-curricular activities that bring students satisfaction. The 'wasted time' is supposed to be spent in the company of tutors or self-study. This is a misguided step in parenting which stems from the belief that the intelligent brain needs to be nurtured independent of the emotional brain. When students don't do well in studies, many parents and teachers believe that students should be denied extra-curricular activities, and they should be disciplined, punished, cloistered and their energies channelled solely towards studies. It is wrong to slam doors on those abilities where children take pride in their success. Parents, teachers and social scientists will need to learn new skills to guide students in channelling the energies from things they enjoy doing, to attempting doing those things in which they find no joy or recognition.

Stimulate Happiness

My experience of working with toddlers, preteens and teens for over three decades, points out that the emotional brain is not only dominant but also is superior to the intelligent brain. The emotional (mammalian) brain developed many million years before the intelligent (neo cortex) brain evolved. The emotional brain not only ignites and controls the intelligent brain to a large extent, but it can also shut down the intelligent brain from responding positively. In highly emotional people, the emotional brain may send impulses of prejudice or indifference to the intelligent brain. The intelligent brain processes whatever data is sent to it after the emotional brain filters it. If the data is filtered through negative feelings, the students may take a dislike to the subject and the intelligent brain finds the data tedious to understand. Similarly, when the intelligent brain processes data that was filtered positively by the emotional brain, the student may take keen interest in the subject, learn it quickly and enjoy it thoroughly. By stimulating children to possess happy dispositions you will not only de-stress them but also make them brainy.

Armed with this information, we can use the emotional brain to prod the intelligent brain into action when it 'naps.' If we use this knowledge to our advantage, a lot of average and below average students will benefit immensely. Children, who are weak in maths, should be encouraged to take up music classes so that the music pathways in the brain will stimulate the math pathways. The ability to read music notes will help students to improve their understanding of math problems. (See chapter 10, *Accelerate Your Study Engine through Music*). To achieve such changes, parents and educators may need to radically change their focus – ensure the emotional well-being of children rather than hound students to cram academics. The happier the kids are, the more willingly they will give themselves completely to other disciplines, including studies. Isn't it the same with grown-ups? When you are happy with your boss or colleagues, you contribute more to the well-being of the establishment than you would otherwise.

Laughter, the Best Medicine

Introduce laughter in your homes. Many grown-ups have forgotten how to laugh. Some snigger, others force a smile, while some laugh artificially like the villains laugh in the movies. To laugh freely means you have to laugh like little children who laugh spontaneously. When you laugh freely, your children will also laugh with you spontaneously. Happy children grow up to be happy, generous adults. Cranky children become cranky, self-centred adults. Toddlers, who whimper, whine and howl, usually end up as whiners and gripers when they are adults. Make it a habit to fill your mind with positive ideas and happy thoughts and your home with spontaneous laughter. Each day, make it your goal to spread a positive aura around you. Begin and end each day by stimulating happy thoughts in your children so that they develop jovial dispositions.

Happy Feelings Flow from Your Brain

What makes humans so different from each other? We are so much alike and yet so different. We share common similarities and yet have essential dissimilarities. Like any computer hardware, all humans share a hi-tech, state-of-the-art computer hardware. What make us so different from the others is the way we think, feel and act. This we attribute to our personal highly sophisticated software. According to Michael Anthony in *How to be Happy*, what most individuals don't realise is that the power of the brain or the computer's hardware varies according to the chemistry of one's brain. You can dramatically increase the power and efficiency of your brain or personal computer by optimising the chemistry of its cranial fluid.

Your brain secretes chemicals corresponding to the positive and negative thoughts. The chemical composition of the cranial fluid from your brain determines how well you perform in everything. For instance, students who enter the examination hall feeling fear and anxiety will perform poorly compared to students who enter the examination hall feeling confident. You may want to know why feelings of fear and anxiety make you perform poorly. Compare your hi-tech, state-of-the-art computer brain to that of a car which runs on lead-free petrol. If you use leaded petrol, which contains chemical contaminants, to run the car, your car engine will sputter and may cause engine damage. Similarly, when you entertain negative thoughts you put 'leaded' fluid into your brain. When this cranial chemical, the contaminated leaded fluid, flows through the neurotransmitters in your hi-tech, state-of-the-art computerised brain, your systems sputter and the output is negative. On the other hand, when you are positive and operating confidently, your brain secretes 'unleaded' cranial chemicals and your ability to perform excels.

Dopamine and Cortisol

Among the many chemicals that the brain secretes as cranial fluids, there are two fluids that either may propel us to soar high or pull us down. The two cranial fluids – dopamine and cortisol – directly affect our emotions since they regulate moods and are responsible for our mood swings. Dopamine is the fluid that keeps us happy. Have you felt contentment after eating say, dark chocolate, ice cream or something you were craving for? Have you felt contentment, say after a good round of exercise? Contentment is the mood of satisfaction that you felt. On eating these foods or breaking into a sweat after doing some rigorous exercises, your brain releases dopamine into the bloodstream and a feeling of relaxation, satiation and well-being spreads throughout the body.

Then there is cortisol, the cranial fluid that fuels your anger, stress and all the negativity inside you. Every time you feel hostile, stressed or pressured, cortisol is produced by the brain and released through millions of neurotransmitters into the bloodstream. Can you imagine people who are regularly depressed, stressed or angry and the volume of cortisol the brain produces for days on end? It's like chain smokers with nicotine in their blood or alcoholics and drug addicts with poisonous chemicals lacing the bloodstream! On the other hand, there are people with happy dispositions and positive thoughts. Their brains produce ample supplies of dopamine. It's like driving your swanky car on a tank full of high-octane fuel.

Get Rid of Negativity

Your mind and body work in sync with each other. Your brain receives all the data from the five senses and acts upon it. You've seen sportspersons who've had a bad season of losses. Watch them enter the games field. As you watch their body language, you can almost tell what their thoughts are. They badly want to win the game but the fear of losing another game, causes their brains to secrete chemicals that immediately impair their performance. And, then you see the team that has had a great season of wins. You will see the players walk on the games field like champions, their body language buoyant with confidence, as they smile and wave at the audience, chest out, head high and raring to go. The opportunity of winning another game causes their brains to secrete chemicals that bring on a rush of high exhilaration and immediately boost their spirits. They feel absolutely charged; ready to trounce the enemy and grab the trophy.

We can learn from such examples of sportspersons, through whose body language we can read the messages of positivity and negativity. Learn to interpret non-verbal messages and signals so that you can receive positive messages and reject the negative ones. You need to learn ways to stamp out all negativity from your minds and fill your thoughts with positivity. You can train your mind and body to stay positive and happy. Go ahead; give yourself a pep talk each morning of every day. The first thing you need to do in the morning when you wake up is, stand in front of a mirror, smile at yourself and consciously tell yourself aloud, "I, (state your name) am a happy person." "I am very happy to be alive today." "I believe in myself." "Today, I will spread happiness to people around me." "I believe I can do it." "I will not let myself down." "I am here for a purpose." "I will try to achieve my goals today." After having fed yourself a generous dose of positivity, your next move is, walk, talk and act like a happy winner. Put a song in your heart, a tune on your lips and a spring in your step, as you prepare to grab the day and spread the aura of positivity around you.

Staying Happy and Positive

To keep the mercury of joy soaring high, the dopamine fluid has to flow uninterruptedly. As a beginner, every effort you make to be a positive person must be a conscious one. It will take time before the positive inputs you consciously plant in your brain become second nature to you. In the meantime, let us look at an analogy. What do the banks ATM counters do? They have the ability and the capacity to process ATM/debit cards and dole out money. The catchword is 'process.' Consider yourself as the bank with an ATM counter. To stay on top, your ATM machine needs to increase its processing abilities to perform better academically and socially. Your ATM machine also needs to increase its processing capacity to stay happy in most situations and positive in all situations. You can do it by consciously adjusting the chemistry of your brain's cranial fluid. To understand how this is done, let us take one step at a time. First, your brain responds depending on the data it receives from the five sense organs. Next, the chemical compounds of the cranial fluids, which control your moods, are formed by the quality of your sleep, diet, exercise and environment. These external factors influence your thoughts (positive or negative) and these thoughts are fed to the brain. You could choose to stay happy and function positively or you could choose to stay depressed and function negatively. The external factors, such as sleep, diet, exercise and environment, influence the five senses that formulate thought, which in turn will affect the release of the brain's cranial fluids – dopamine and cortisol.

Sleep. Your body needs its full quota of sleep so that it can rejuvenate itself, re-build spent cells and eliminate the toxins. During your waking hours, your five senses had registered thousands of experiences. While you asleep, your brain stays awake, processing all the information it received when you were awake. It's like seeing a movie in replay mode. The brain files and catalogues all the 'impressionable' data for future use.

Diet. Everything you eat and drink is reduced to chemicals that affect your performance, moods and feelings. Skipping meals or overeating affect the body and mind. Skipping meals may make you restless and irritable, while overeating may make you sluggish. Humans are designed to live on natural foods with proper quantity and distribution of protein, carbohydrates and fat in their diet. Eat wisely and in moderation. Do not become neurotic about what you eat. Staying happy is far more important than what you eat, even though what you eat is important. (*How To Be Happy*, Michael Anthony).

Exercise. If people thought the 1970s were fast, then by those standards 2008 should be rated as super-fast. Are we running faster now than before? Perhaps mentally, but not physically. Physically we have become sluggish and out of shape, while mentally we are continuously running, hopping, skipping, jumping loops, practically and figuratively. With so much strain, stress and pressure at work, home, school and at the social level, the result is that the cranial fluids we generate contain negative chemicals. Our bodies were designed for physical exertion. Earlier, people ate food by farming, hunting and fishing. We don't. To stay fit in mind and body we may have to commit ourselves to a regimen of intense exercises. Daily vigorous exercise along with chores (choosing those which will make you sweat profusely) will not only knock off the toxins from the body but will also generate the secretion of dopamine, which in turn will result in happy feelings and a positive attitude.

Environment. You may huff and puff your toxins out while you exercise vigorously; you may eat right and sleep tight;

you may give yourself a dazzling pep talk every morning; but if the people you are surrounded by are filled with negativity, there is precious little you can do from feeling despondent, depressed, worried, anxious, sad, or miserable. Some people are fault-finders. They are angry at the world. They are less benign in their view of others. They will fault family, relatives, friends, teachers, career, colleagues, politics, media, movies, *et al.* They see the world as ugly, depressing and hostile. If you are in such an environment, it will be difficult for you to stay cheerful and optimistic. Their negative words, actions and thoughts will adversely affect you. But there is a way out. Create your own environment. The old saying is, you can choose your friends but you're stuck with your relatives. So, go ahead and choose happy people for friends. Make it a point to associate only with positive people. Choose cheerful people for company. Have a larger circle of friends. The only time you should associate with negative people is when you are trying to help them. Before meeting them, consciously tell yourself that it's your mission to spread the aura of positivity. If negativity is contagious, so is positivity. With your strong positive aura, the negativity will not touch you. On the contrary, negative persons will be touched by your optimism.

Your happiness and success depends entirely on increasing the positive chemistry of your cranial fluid so that your brain can perform more efficiently. This is not classified rocket science but common knowledge that positive thoughts will trigger the release of positive chemicals in the brain. This, in turn, will ignite the power of your brain to function at optimum levels. Difficult problems get solved when the mind is fed with positivity. Similarly, negative thoughts will trigger the release of negative chemicals in the brain. This, in turn, will make a person feel tense, listless, defeated and depressed. Your happiness and success depends on this age-old simple but profound concept – *Don't Worry, Be Happy!*

Points to Remember

1. The emotional (mammalian) brain evolved before the intelligent (neo-cortex) brain. Since emotions control intelligence in many ways, it is extremely important to ignite the students' weak zones through their strengths.
2. When the emotional brain is stressed or upset, it sends negative impulses to the intelligent brain. This makes students plough through pages and pages of books without understanding what they study.
3. Dopamine is the 'happy' hormone and cortisol is the 'stress' hormone. Avoid stressing students; a happy environment stimulates the release of dopamine fluid to enable them to excel.
4. To stay happy every day, remind yourself in the mirror through the morning pep talk that you are a happy person and you believe in staying happy throughout the day.
5. The brain controls the body and the body feeds the brain. For the brain to function at peak levels, the body should feed the brain with quality sleep habits, regular vigorous exercises and games, a balanced diet and a cluster of happy people for company.

7

Homework is Not *Injurious* to Health

Salient Features

The foundation for good study habits is set as early as the toddler age. Unfortunately, parents remain ignorant on the purpose and importance of homework. The students 'occupation' is to study. The positive reinforcement of such occupation by parents will help motivate students to complete their homework. Teachers should not assign homework as punishment nor should they withdraw homework as a reward. Homework assignments should be corrected, and the notebooks must be handed over to the students while the matter is still fresh in their minds. Homework should be treated as an extension of the lessons learnt in school. Concepts taught in school are firmly grasped when students read, write and revise those concepts at home. Parents ought to believe in the importance of homework. Students do well in academics when parents create an environment at home where fixed hours are routinely dedicated to home study, free from family distractions.

As children, most of us went through the rigours of being forced to eat foods we hated. Oh yes, we argued, cried and ranted against eating, while our parents extolled its virtues and sternly told us how good it was for us. After succumbing to pressure, didn't we linger endlessly over the food, hoping it would vanish somehow? If you can recall those childhood memories, you will understand why children find homework an imposition on their 'fun' time. They find homework so distasteful that they argue, cry, rant and hide it with the hope that it would somehow disappear.

Laying the 'Homework' Foundation

Just as the foundation for good eating habits are set early, so also the foundation for good study habits should be set at an early age, for instance say, when the child is about four years old. For toddlers, play is a tool for learning new skills. Parents should explore play-way methods to absorb the child in completing 'homework' such as, colouring, pasting, pattern writing, browsing through books, building blocks – generally do all the things that toddlers enjoy doing. Such activities should be done daily at a fixed time, say after lunch, and in a fixed place, away from electronic distractions and family intrusions. In doing so, you would have set the foundation of learning for a lifetime. In all probability, parents will face no problem on the homework front once toddlers get into the habit of studying on their own. When they grow up to be pre-teens and teens they will automatically reach out for the school bag after lunch and complete their homework – even without parental supervision. Unfortunately, only a small percentage of parents would have initiated this study habit in their children. Most parents remain ignorant on the purpose and importance of homework; they consider homework a punishment. They open the school bags with heavy hearts, hoping there would be no homework. They breathe a sign of relief when they find no homework because without the burden of homework, the child is free to play all evening. Or, is it the other way around, without homework, parents are free to pursue their own agendas? You will often hear parents whine and complain about homework. At times their whines are justified, and at times, not.

When Homework is Meaningless

Teachers should never assign homework as punishment, nor should they use "No Homework" as a reward. Homework gets a bad name when teachers:

(a) Say something to the effect, "since this class is judged the best in the inter-class competition, you will have no homework for tomorrow!"

(b) Assign volumes of homework to keep students 'busy' on the weekends.

(c) Some teachers, under the guise of homework, 'off-load' the syllabus over to the students. Teachers assign untaught curriculum as homework and never teach the same in class again. Students are expected to learn new concepts either on their own or through the help from parents or tutors.

Teachers should realise that the purpose of homework is to 'revise and practice' what was taught in class, not to cover new territory. But when homework is assigned recklessly and students spend frustrating study hours unable to complete those assignments, it is only justifiable for parents and students to whine and groan under the burden of academics. Also, there are teachers who are liberal in handing out homework, and quick to punish students for failing to complete the homework on time. Unfortunately, those same teachers rarely correct the assignments on time. Some brazenly 'initial' the assignments without reading the text or making corrections. Students who apply themselves assiduously and commit valuable time to completing homework, are denied the opportunity to learn from their mistakes and improve their knowledge of the subject. It is common knowledge that students use their homework books as reference material to study for tests and exams. The errors committed in the homework copies are the errors they repeat in the test or exam papers, which pull them down for no fault of theirs. Indeed, students suffer a colossal waste of time, energy and talent due to oversight and negligence on the part of teachers.

Believing in Homework

Ask students, "What is your occupation?" Most of them will answer they have no occupation. But one in a hundred may surprise you and say, "My occupation is to study." This belief, that they have an occupation, radically propels students to handle serious responsibilities. In fact, many parents, who are the primary educators of children, don't believe that students have an occupation. Childhood is the time to play, and youth is the time to have fun. Many parents are of the belief that all the education children receive should be contained within the school premises. Children should return home from school, free of books and homework. This basic misconception is the foundation for poor study habits. When home study is considered a punishment, how can students relish the idea of studying? Can you imagine parents rushing off to work day-after-day as punishment? If you hate your work so much, how can children enjoy theirs? When 'occupation' is considered a punishment, personal growth is the first casualty. On the other hand, when the concept of study as an 'occupation' is positively reinforced by parents and teachers, students' approach to study will automatically be motivated with a sense of responsibility.

Parental Support

Just as parents and teachers train themselves professionally to function competently in their occupation, so also students must be exposed to a professional approach to home study. The exercise will definitely improve the students' competency in their occupation. You don't instil good study habits by punishing students for the behaviour you don't want; instead, you do it by reinforcing the habits you want. 'Professional Approach' to home study would imply the following:

a) Be positive about homework. Tell children how important schoolwork is. The attitude you express about homework will be the attitude your child acquires.

b) Teach children time management in practical ways. Parents should help students organise a timetable for daily home study. *(Read chapter 8, Study Smart and Get to a Flying Start).*

c) Ensure a distraction-free environment to do homework. People moving in and out of the room while the child is studying, should be restricted; (treat the study zone like the hospital ICU). Switch off the television, computer, telephone, music systems and all that generates distractions.

d) Make sure that the materials your child will need – textbooks, notebooks, pencils, eraser, sharpener, dictionary, bottle of water and tumbler are within arm's reach before sitting to study.

e) Guide students to prioritise – study the tough and difficult subjects first, and the easy subjects last. Also, some homework has to be completed immediately, while other homework has to be submitted after the weekend.

f) Ensure students have time for daily revision of what was covered in class.

g) Supervise the 'reading ahead' habit in order to familiarise oneself with matter to be covered the next day in class.

h) When your child asks for help, provide guidance not answers. Giving answers will never help the child study independently nor will the child learn quickly. Too much help teaches the child to switch off difficult subjects because someone else will handle them.

i) Use the power of praise to motivate; parents should consistently praise their children for the effort they put into their homework and not just praise them for correctness. Letting children know that you appreciate the time and effort they put into home study every day, works as a powerful motivation for kids to perform to the best of their abilities.

j) Be around when the child needs you, but don't hover over the child's work, inspecting every punctuation mark. Never do the child's homework even when you are in a hurry.

k) Stay in touch with your child's teacher, be it nursery school, primary school, middle school, secondary school or higher secondary school. When you make an effort to talk to your child's teachers, your child realises that both home and school work as a team.

Get the Most out of Homework

How much time should be spent on doing homework per subject, you may ask? The thumb rule should be ten to fifteen minutes of homework per subject and not more than four subjects per day. Teachers are expected to be 'time managers' who should determine how much time students must ideally spend doing a particular homework. Each subject teacher should co-ordinate with colleagues in the staff room on the amount of homework they allot each class. This co-ordination will enable students to devote, say one hour at home for doing homework each day. The second hour of study can be fruitfully spent revising, outlining and reading ahead for the next day's class. Homework becomes meaningful when teachers:

(a) Inform parents of the importance of the homework that is assigned.
(b) Reinforce skills introduced in the classroom.
(c) Promote independent in-depth study of the chosen topics.
(d) Promote wise and orderly use of time outside school hours.
(e) Follow up in class the previous day's assignment.
(f) When making corrections, point out errors along with strengths. (Positive remarks will encourage students to work harder). In doing so, teachers not only check homework but also evaluate it.
(g) Return corrected copies to students within three days (while the matter is hopefully still fresh in their minds). When schools make it a policy that teachers must return corrected copies within three days, they will automatically lessen the volume of homework they allot.

Play Smart, Study Smarter

Students who bring home poor grades, term after term, are generally treated as duffers at school and at home. The hard truth is that they are not duffers. These same students, who get written off as duffers, often shine out in activities where their talents are rarely recognised or appreciated. But they do poorly in academics. They fail because at school they are taught, nay hounded by uninspiring teachers. At home, they are nurtured, nay policed by uninspiring parents. Parents may lack the spirit of enterprise but they want their children to be enterprising. Many teachers and parents openly admit they are computer dinosaurs. Their minds are shut to modern electronic gadgets and facilities. While parents use ancient parenting (spare the rod and spoil the child) technique, teachers use archaic teaching methods (teaching the way they were taught, say two decades ago). Yet, both teams place unrealistically high expectations on students' performance in academics. On the other hand, there are parents and teachers who have a natural flair or instinct to discipline themselves, even to the point of altering their personal lifestyles to mould, guide and direct the lives of children under their care. Such parents and teachers are driven by passion and dedication to give children as many opportunities as possible to express themselves through music, dance, arts and beyond, despite the burden of academics. These fortunate students learn at a very early age without stress or pressure, the importance of time management, commitment, dedication, responsibility and a lot more. Many such students come home from school, wash up, have a hot lunch and immediately open their school bags and begin doing their homework. By evening time, they are free to pursue games and hobbies. Indeed, from the time that they had breakfast till the time they have their supper, they cover a lot of ground every day, moving from one activity to another. Following such busy routines do not break the backs of students; hence, there is no reason to believe that applying oneself consistently to the routine of home study along with the pursuit of hobbies will be injurious to health.

Points to Remember

1. Fixed time for home study must be inculcated in students at the toddler age.
2. Homework assignments become meaningless when untaught curriculum is off-loaded on students, or when homework copies are not corrected on time for students to learn from their mistakes.
3. Parents must welcome homework as an opportunity to revise class work and not curse it.
4. Teachers should use homework as a tool to reinforce in-depth learning of concepts taught in class.
5. Parents and teachers have to reinvent themselves in order to reach out to students, and bring out the best in them through the pursuit of academics and hobbies.

8

Study Smart and Get to a Flying Start

Salient Features

Many students look lost and confused when they sit to study. They would rather be busy doing other things than pretend to show how busy they are studying. Students who are disinterested in academics usually display behaviour problems in school and at home. One of the best ways to motivate students is to nurture their dignity and self-esteem through household chores which will bring them instant appreciation. Recognition for their actions will draw them closer to you when they feel how deeply you care about them. When you are able to arouse feelings of love and care in the children, the rest follows easily. Since studying is bound in routine and structures, start with the things-to-do list, followed by fixed times to sleep and wake up, fixed meal times and gradually stick to a daily timetable. New research shows how complex matters when read the night before are comprehended faster the following day. This knowledge, along with practical habits to develop a good memory, will help students to get to a flying start.

In my book, *Love Without Spoiling, Discipline Without Nagging*, I had dedicated a section to 'Study Skills.' In this book, I will show pre-teens and teens ways to academic success through smart study habits. Habits form the backbone of success. Slothful habits make for a weak backbone, and a weak backbone crumbles under the backpack of academic burden. Structured habits make for a strong backbone and a strong backbone carries the academic backpack as though there is no burden.

I conduct regular workshops for pre-teens and teens. These workshops are divided into four sessions each, of three months duration. Sessions run as follows: (i) Spoken and Written English, (ii) Effective Study Habits, (iii) Public Speaking and Leadership, and (iv) Personality Development. Within two months of attending the workshops, students begin to display positive changes in attitude and behaviour. The parents are pleased not only because the nagging at home drops dramatically but also because the teachers in school share their appreciation. Is it possible that habits ingrained, say for ten to sixteen years, could change within a span of two months, you may want to know? Let us look into the finer aspects of how pre-teens and teens are able to change their habits to improve grades so that you can guide your pre-teens and teens to do likewise.

Instil Self-motivation

It is an inner drive or force that makes a person want to perform certain actions, no matter what the cost. In my workshops, I first reinforce in the students the primary goal, that is, their only job at this juncture in life is to study, nothing else. Now comes the moment of truth. How do you make them believe in this goal and work to achieve this goal? They need a motivating environment, an environment that will remind them daily of their duties. It is important at this point to introduce them to an environment of structures as they begin to set some basic goals. To plant the seeds of motivation in their hearts and minds, I appeal to their sense of pride, dignity and self-esteem so that, without being told or reminded by others, they passionately strive to achieve those goals. Incidentally, study habits are not *per se* among the basic goals we set, though academic success is the primary goal. Among the basic goals, students learn ways to release dopamine and shut off cortisol. (See chapter 6, *Positive Juices Stimulate the Brain*). During the first two weeks of the workshop, students learn to focus on nurturing positive thoughts, develop a positive aura and spread positivity at home and in school. Assignments are designed to work as reinforcement tools to achieve those goals. The sessions begin with group discussions. Students are least inhibited when speaking their minds. In the group discussions, students would tell the group about certain old habits they had stopped because they were detrimental to their goals; some old habits they continued since they were in consonance with their goals; and some new habits they began which they considered would lead them to their goals. Hearing each other's experiences, those who had achieved twenty percent changes in behaviour were inspired to achieve more, and those who had achieved forty percent also wanted to achieve more. Within two months into the workshop, the students' positive actions automatically rose beyond their parents and teachers expectations. It is true, behaviour does influence academic performance and *vice versa*.

Embrace Structure as a Lifestyle

Structured habits are the backbone to success. Some experts who work with children are of the opinion that children should grow up free of structures. They plant those seeds in the parents' minds when the kids are toddlers – the most impressionable age. As a result, in the confusion of what is right and what is wrong, children develop erratic sleep patterns; become fussy eaters; restless and fidgety, unable to stay focused on any one activity; lack respect for grown-ups and throw tantrums among other things. By the time they are six years old, parents give up on them; in some cases, parents threaten them that if they don't behave themselves they will be sent to a boarding school. The ultimate punishment; being banished to a boarding school is supposed to work as a detriment to bad behaviour. If you want kids to behave well and study well, then don't punish them with banishment. There is an easier way to do it. Start the day by

1) set limits and boundaries (activities should be time-bound), 2) make a list of things-to-do, and 3) make a list of things-NOT-to-do. At the end of the day, review points 1, 2, and 3. This exercise, when followed every day, will give children direction and structure. Why are parents misguided on structured upbringing is a baffling issue. When we are surrounded by structure, why can't we be groomed to blend with nature? There is structure in the universe, the planets, the seasons, the oceans, nature, creatures, and everywhere. Why do our children have to grow up without structure? Victims of unstructured lives find it an uphill task structuring their lives as grown-ups. Most blame it on their genes or circumstances.

Sleep Structure

Sleep relaxes and refreshes the mind and body. When you deprive the body of sleep due to late night study, you suffer from brain fatigue. Thinking becomes disorganised and memory gets impaired. On the other hand, on school days, students usually go to bed and wake up at fixed times. But on holidays, they sleep late and wake up late. They believe that weekends are meant to laze around. The opposite is true. A good night's sleep of eight hours is necessary for memory consolidation and concentration. Dr Pierre Marquet at the University in Belgium, after conducting extensive research concluded that regions in the brain which were being used for learning a new task, were the same regions that 'mulled' the matter over during the night, enabling students easy understanding of the matter the following day. It showed that the brain kept on learning the task while the students were fast asleep. Students should take advantage of this research and read difficult subjects before going to bed. After reading, they should go to bed; not watch television, surf the net, or else they will lose this unique advantage.

Time Structure

There are only so many hours in a day, a week and a term. You cannot change the number of hours, but you can decide how to best use them. To be successful in school, you must carefully manage your study time. It is advisable that on school days, students set aside approximately two to three hours for home study. On weekends and holidays, students should programme approximately four to five hours each day for home study. To gain optimum mileage from home study, making and following a time table is a good habit. To help you plan your time efficiently, you will need three kinds of timetables: (i) Term Planner, (ii) Weekly Schedule, and (iii) Daily Timetable.

(i) **Trimester/Semester Term Planner**. Stationery shops may have term calendars and year planner charts. You can buy or make one. Use coloured felt pens to record your planned school activities, assignment deadlines, unit tests and exams; also list out-of-school activities, such as festivals, family and social commitments. After recording important dates, stick this chart prominently above your study desk. You now have an overall view of the extra busy times and can organise around them.

(ii) **Weekly Schedule**. You need copies of blank weekly timetable sheets, in one-hour blocks. Each Sunday evening, before the week begins, with an eye on the *Term Planner*, prepare your *Weekly Schedule*, Mondays to Sundays. Update it as the week goes on. Here is what to do:

   a) record your daily classes;
   b) enter things to be done for the coming week from your *Term Planner*;
   c) review your class notes from the previous week to see if you need to add any school activities;
   d) record extra coaching you will take in studies, games, etc.
   e) add any out-of-school activities in which you will be involved during the week;
   f) include time periods for completing assignments, working on projects, and studying for tests. These

time periods may be during the school day, right after school, evenings and weekends.

It is recommended that students honestly devote approximately four hours per week to each important subject. *Your timetable should be subject oriented.* Divide your time into subject blocks, such as maths, science, language, social studies. There will be times when some subjects may need more time than others. Some subject blocks may require thirty minutes, while others may require one to two hours. What you do in these blocks should largely be determined by assignment demands. It is advisable that you try to keep the time period for each subject constant.

(iii) Daily Timetable. Each evening before going to bed, students will prepare the *Daily Timetable* for the next day. The following day, they will put a *tick-mark symbol* next to each item when it is accomplished. To prepare the *Daily Timetable,* enter the bedtime and wake-up time (students should sleep for eight to ten hours every night). Next, enter the things to do for the coming day from the *Weekly Schedule.* Use a red marker to enter the things that still need to be accomplished from the previous day's timetable. It is extremely important that each student should plan and set aside time by using different coloured markers for (a) to revise the day's subjects and class notes and (b) do the homework assignments in the order of importance. Lastly, enter any out-of-school activities (social outings) in which the student will be involved the next day.

Students will need ready and quick access to the *Daily Timetable*. It will be impractical if they put it on a chart and stick it to the study table. The *Daily Timetable* is their lifeline to success; hence, they will need to keep it handy and accessible. Get a hardcover notebook and enter the *Daily Timetable* as in a diary. Learn to prioritise by working out the order of importance. Tough subjects need immediate attention when the brain is not tired, while the least important subjects can be listed at the bottom of the priority list. Lastly, before sitting to study, always refer to the *Daily Timetable* for direction – it is every student's lifeline to success.

To develop the habit of structuring time efficiently, make sure that the *Weekly Schedule* has more details than the *Term Planner* and similarly the *Daily Timetable* has more details than the *Weekly Schedule*. Students who grow into the habit to honestly follow the *Daily Timetable* without skipping a day will obviously become efficient time managers for the rest of their lives.

Healthy Habits Stimulate Memory

What is memory? Memory is the mental activity of recalling information that you have learned or experienced. Memory can be short-term or long-term. In short-term memory, your brain stores information for a few seconds or a few minutes. Such memory is fragile and it is meant to be. You don't need to remember the numbers of every phone call you made, nor do you need to store in your memory every word you read in the newspaper or what you saw and heard on television. If that would happen, you would suffer from "data overload." Information gets stored in the long-term memory when it is reinforced by a conscious or unconscious effort to retain it. Matters of interest, need, desire, want, importance get stored in the long-term memory bank. If you think you have poor memory, it could be because of disinterest and certain personal habits that obstruct your brain from effectively processing information. Some students can remember sports scores of several years and other such data which parents and teachers consider unimportant. But those same students find memorising math and science formulae extremely difficult. It's not due to the lack of brainpower but merely because of the lack of interest in math and science. Now, help is at hand. If you practice healthy habits, you can improve your ability to concentrate and retain information.

You heard the old saying, "Repetition is the mother of learning." Now, recall the time you attended a small party and one of the guests kept the audience rolling in laughter as he reeled off joke after joke. You envied the person's skill; he was able to graphically recreate and tell so many jokes, especially when you are unable to remember a single one. When you told a joke, either you revealed the punchline right at the beginning or simply forgot it. The way to remember jokes is to repeat them to someone as soon as possible. The key word is, 'as soon as possible.' The more often you repeat the jokes the more comfortable you get in telling them. If you stop telling jokes, you will forget them. The same principle of memory recall applies to students. If they want to remember what they studied, students will have to repeat their story to someone soon or else they will forget the matter they learnt. In short, in order to remember something, you have to regularly remind yourself about it and keep telling it as often as you can. Another word for this activity is 'revision.'

Healthy Lifestyle Builds Good Memory

Exercise Daily

Doing exercises daily doesn't require a gym. You need the will to find a way. Running or jogging on the pavements or in the parks is good enough. Spot jogging in your room, say for fifteen to thirty minutes every day is an excellent tonic to refresh yourself. Playing basketball, soccer, hockey and other games that make you huff, puff and sweat for an hour are also excellent health tonics. Your exercise should be strenuous which increases the heartbeat and you break into a sweat as you pant for air. This not only increases oxygen to the brain, but it also reduces the risk of disorders that lead to memory loss, such as obesity, diabetes and cardiovascular disease. (If you subject your body to substance abuse, like tobacco, alcohol and drugs, you run the risk of slowing down your brain functions). Daily strenuous exercises release dopamine, which rejuvenates the body, protects brain cells and improves concentration and memory.

Deep Uninterrupted Sleep.

Students who suffer from brain fatigue, catch only a few hours of sleep at night, and tend to nap in the day. Researcher Sara C. Mednick in *Nature Neuroscience* wrote an article called, *The Restorative Effect of Naps on Perceptual Deterioration*. She had found that students, whose sleep patterns were erratic, developed poor concentration levels because too much effort on the same day was harmful to learning. When the brain is tired, it starts to shut down to protect itself from data-overload. What can you do to keep the brain alert? Sleep is the best stimulant. Students need at least eight hours of deep, uninterrupted sleep every night. The brain never sleeps; but the brain requires the body systems to shut down (sleep) in order to sort things out, put all the material learned into mental files and catalogues, and store them in long-term memory banks.

Food to Feed the Brain

You may already know that a balanced diet contains fruits, vegetables, whole grains, eggs and 'healthy' fats. Some nutritionists guide parents on the types of foods they should stock at home and feed the kids. Children, who are restless, listless, unable to sleep at nights, have poor concentration, and are hyperactive may need a change in dietary habits. Some foods, when digested and broken down into chemicals, may either make children restless or listless or hyperactive or passive. You have to know what foods to give your children and when to feed them, since foods affect moods. Be diet savvy. Provide the right diet which will boost energy, increase the ability to concentrate and keep the mind alert. Research indicates that the following nutrients nurture and stimulate most of the brain functions:

a) **Foods that contain B vitamins** (B6, B12, and folic acid): Spinach and other dark leafy greens, broccoli, asparagus, strawberries, melons, citrus fruits, soybeans, black beans and other legumes.

b) **Foods that contain oxidants** (Vitamin C, vitamin E, and beta carotene): All types of berries (red, black, yellow, brown, blue, purple), sweet potatoes, beetroot, red tomatoes, spinach, broccoli, green tea, nuts and seeds, citrus fruits, liver.

c) **Foods that contain Omega-3 fatty acids:** Walnuts and walnut oil, fish – salmon, tuna, herring, mackerel, cod, and mostly fish that have a black-blue sheen on the skin; the dark layer of fat under the skin of the fish is very rich in Omega-3 fatty acids. The Omega-3 fatty acids are concentrated in the brain and are associated with cognitive function. They protect against inflammation and high cholesterol.

It would be worth learning a little about *Ayurveda,* an approximately 5000-year old science of India. A study of body types such as *Pita, Vata* and *Kapha* will guide you on the diet to be followed to maintain physical and mental agility and good health.

Daily Routine

There is no substitute for daily routine. Students, who are not exposed to a life of routine at the toddler age, find it extremely difficult to discipline themselves as pre-teens and teens. Unfortunately, there is no substitute for routine. If students desire to succeed then they will have to pay the price of committing themselves to follow a structured routine every day. A commitment to routine means, students will have to train themselves to exercise at fixed times, study at fixed times, eat everything in moderation but always eat at fixed times, sleep and wake up at fixed times. If you look at the lives of sportspersons, business leaders and those who are in the millionaires' list of successful people, you will see that they are married to a life of routine. Dame Routine is waiting in the aisle, ready to take you by the hand and lead you to success. Are you ready and willing to be led by Dame Routine on the road to success?

Points to Remember

1. Students must be guided to be self-motivated so that they set short-term goals. Rather than focus on intellectual achievements, set performance targets on chores like personal grooming, having neat and tidy habits, packing the school bag, sleeping and waking on time, etc. Constant appreciation of their achievements will feed their desire to perform positive deeds regularly.
2. Students slip down the slopes of failure because they have never been used to following a structured routine. Children who follow daily routines are able to achieve a lot more in a short while than those who while away time not knowing what to do and at what time.
3. Success depends on how students manage their time. Parents have to help students organise their time efficiently through the *Term Planner*, *Weekly Schedule* and the *Daily Timetable*.
4. Disinterest in particular subjects is the cause for poor memory. The brain has two types of memory banks: short-term and long-term. Material that is understood and retained is stored in the long-term memory bank.
5. Healthy habits are very essential for a good memory. Habits that aid memory are, sound sleep, a fixed routine and health foods to feed the brain, such as B vitamins, oxidants, and Omega 3 fatty acids.

9

What is Reading without Understanding and Remembering?

Salient Features

So much time, effort and energy get wasted when students are unable to grasp and retain what they read. Reading to retain needs special skills, unlike reading novels or the newspaper. The special skills are divided into two areas: physical environment and the SQ3R Method of Reading. When reading to retain what has been studied, the correct physical environment is very important, such as reading in a noise-free area, free from interruptions and distractions, with the study desk correctly positioned and stacked with study materials. A comfortable study chair, with proper lighting and room temperature makes for an ideal physical environment for reading to remember. The SQ3R Reading Method – Survey, Question, Read, Recite and Review are laid down in detail. Students can easily practice the SQ3R reading method which is followed in many parts of the world to increase and improve reading skills, comprehension and retention of what is read.

People go to restaurants to eat and drink. Can you imagine sitting in a restaurant for several hours without a crumb to eat or a drop to drink? A sheer waste of time, you will say! Similarly, can you imagine students sitting down to read for several hours every day without understanding the meaning of what they read or remember an idea of what they read? You will admit that would be a colossal waste of time!

To instil a lifetime habit of reading, the best format is the 'read aloud' family programme. Read *with* your child as often as you can. Select some age-appropriate reading activity in which the whole family can participate every day. While teens can read aloud drama, poetry and the newspapers, pre-teens can read aloud passages from storybooks. For children to imbibe the habit of serious reading, the best way to start is leisure reading. Through the daily practice of having a family reading hour, you will not only set a good example but also instil a love for reading.

This chapter will show you how to harness your effort, time and energy and make your reading exercises accountable and valuable. What the skin is to the body, reading is to studying. Reading is an intrinsic part of studying, like skin and body. Applying oneself to serious study, demands attentive reading, and students have to get into the habit of reading attentively. To master the art of reading-to-study, students have to realise that reading has two aspects: physical environment and technical know-how and that both are co-related since one compliments the other.

(1) Physical Environment

The main ingredients to read effectively are concentration, attention, interest and focus. These qualities can be achieved provided students have a proper physical environment for such a purpose. Let us take a practical look at the physical environment that is so important for students to study effectively and efficiently. Run a checklist on the following to see if your home supports the physical environment required for reading-to-study:

Studying should be done in a fixed place

Concentration, attention and focus demand that students should not spread themselves over the whole house. They should not flit in and out of rooms or the balcony while reading. Serious study requires a fixed place with appropriate fixtures.

Study time should be free from distractions and interruptions

Reading and distractions don't go hand in hand. Students must have 'zero tolerance' for distractions and interruptions. Move the study desk away from windows and doors and place it against a blank wall. Switch off the cell phone, *ipod*, playstation, television, laptop, computer, radio, MP3 and other gizmos that could interrupt reading-to-study.

Study desk should have all the study materials

The study desk should have the textbooks, reference books, notebooks, dictionary, sharpened pencils, pens, ball pens, eraser, paper, ruler, calculator and every stationery item you will require without the need to leave the room in-between. (No food items should be allowed on the study desk). In case, a student regularly uses the computer for schoolwork, then it should be near the study desk, not in another room.

Comfortable study chair

An uncomfortable chair can cause discomfort and hurt back muscles. The discomfort, which could result in slouching and constantly shifting positions, will affect concentration. A chair that is cosy and snug might induce sleep. Straight-back chairs without arms and light cushioned seats (dining chairs) are ideal as study chairs. They are very functional for reading-to-study. The straight back chairs will not strain the back, and students can sit on them for hours without falling asleep on them.

Adequately lit study area

White fluorescent light is more soothing to the eyes than yellow light. The light bulbs should be so placed that shadows don't fall over the books when reading. If the lighting is dim, students will strain their eyes, which in turn will slow down the reading.

Comfortable room temperature

If the feet and fingers feel chilled in winters, it will badly affect concentration. On the other hand, in summers, if sweat keeps pouring down the face and back, then concentration suffers. In extreme summers and extreme winters, you may have to control the climate a wee bit so that students are comfortable enough to get on with the reading-to-study, uninterruptedly.

(2) Reading technique in Five Easy Steps

Once you have fixed the physical environment, it's time to arm yourself with the technical know-how of reading to understand and reading to remember. Some parents admit that no matter how diligently children read their assignments, they remember so little. Reading textbooks is not the same as reading novels, or the newspaper. You need a smart technique to read textbooks. To develop result-oriented reading habits, you need a reading method which will quickly increase comprehension and improve the ability to remember. The SQ3R Reading Method is a highly sophisticated and the most effective tool for students. It is used in schools and colleges the world over since it was developed in 1941 by Francis P. Robinson. The abbreviation, SQ3R stands for five steps: (SQ) *Survey, Question* (3R) *Read, Recite and Review.*

To put the SQ3R Reading Method to use, a student's active involvement is the most essential ingredient. Reading is not a passive process but a very active one. To be actively involved in the reading process, the reader has to be very interested in the reading activity. While stress and fatigue may slow down the reader, lack of interest will bring the reading machinery to a grinding halt. Lack of interest in studying is displayed in a number of ways, such as, unable to sit and concentrate even for five minutes; distractions, moodiness, daydreaming, multi-tasking, (trying to show they are busy doing other things); forgetfulness, procrastination, etc.

When a student's job on this planet is to study, then it is imperative that students learn the smartest way to read so that they can quickly understand and retain what they read. The SQ3R Reading Method has five steps; if followed it will help students to enjoy reading and what they read they will understand and retain. Now, let us understand how the five steps can be mastered.

1) Survey: To being with, conduct a survey. Look at the textbook you are holding in your hand. The textbook author has made a conscious effort to select an appropriate tile for the book and the chapter headings. The author has also taken pains to make the information flow in the most logical and natural way by arranging the order in the Table of Contents. Many use the Table of Contents to find something in a hurry. Read carefully the Table of Contents; the different topics will give you an understanding of the subject as a whole. Thereafter, read the Preface. It tells you why the book was written, what the author thinks is important for you to know, and how the information is organised. Make a note of words you do not know and look it up in the dictionary. If the book carries an index at the back, you may want to skim through it. Having done this, you have successfully conducted the *survey*. You are now ready to take the next step.

2) Question: No, don't start reading the first chapter, not yet. At the end of the chapter, most textbooks have questions. Read the questions first. These are sample questions you are required to answer correctly as an affirmation of your comprehension. To understand the importance of this method, soak in this scene. You open one of the kitchen drawers that contain a lot of knick-knacks. You bury your head in the drawer, searching for something. You keep looking into the drawer to find it, and you keep searching and searching for almost half-an-hour without success. Someone asks you, "what are you looking for?" You answer, "I don't know. But, it should be in this drawer. I must find it here." The person is confused, "If you don't know what you're looking for, then how will you find it?" Sadly, this scene is played out in most families, and it is not the kitchen drawer that children stick their heads into. Their heads are bowed over books, which they read for hours on end, day after day, looking for something, hoping to find it without knowing what to look for or what to find. It is common knowledge that if you know what to look for, you will, sooner or later, find it. But if you don't know what you are searching, you will never find it – ever. Each subject chapter is like a drawer, full of clutter. Plunging into the chapter without knowing what to look for is a fruitless and futile endeavour. To study smart, students will have to first formulate questions for each paragraph or section and then attempt reading the chapter. Forming questions will enable students to know what to look for. Once, students know what they are looking for, whether in the paragraph, or in the chapter, they would be empowered by a sense of purpose to read the text. Determination to find answers follows automatically.

Begin writing down questions which are important. How can you tell which question is important when you haven't read the chapter, you may want to know? The brain is not an empty vessel; it has so much information already stored in it. The brain is like a library, with information neatly catalogued and filed. Try and connect some of the stuff you already know with the questions you have read. Now, look at chapter one. It has a title, headings, sub-headings and paragraphs. Change your next move into a game. Introduce a little fun at study time by making wild guesses. Turn the heading or sub-heading, and when there are no headings or sub-headings, turn the first sentence of the paragraph into a question. For instance, take the sub-heading of this section, *Question*. Now turn it into a question, *"What can I find out about the question?"* Next, write down the question in a notebook. By converting sub-headings into questions, students will not only arouse their curiosity to search for answers, but they will automatically stimulate their active involvement, which is called self-motivation. Reading becomes purposeful. The quicker students learn to frame questions the easier the empowerment and motivation to find correct answers. Turning headings into questions could be somewhat easy; reading to find answers to the questions is the exciting journey a student undertakes as the third step.

3) Read: A student has written down a number of questions in the notebook, some from the bottom of the chapter, some from the headings, sub-headings, and others from the first sentences of the paragraphs. All these questions need to be answered. The questions act like a compass, giving the student direction. By searching for answers, the student becomes an active researcher instead of a browser. Browsers waste time and energy and learn almost by accident as they plod through the pages, line after line. Researchers are those who know what to look for and find it. Use a pencil to underline, circle, box only key words, never whole paragraphs. Many students mark too much. Marking should help a student to locate and review important material. Highlight only important points. When students highlight or mark too much, it means they are unable to select main points and important details. The dictionary is a student's companion that must be used to look up unfamiliar words and their meanings. New concepts, words and phrases must be written down in the notebook. (Writing reinforces familiarity with the matter). Then read those words, meanings, phrases and concepts aloud several times for retention. Simultaneously, students should ask themselves, "What does this mean? How does this answer my question? Why is this important? To whom is it important? When? Under what circumstances?" **Caution:** Students need to fully concentrate when they are reading. If they find it difficult to concentrate because they are distracted, disinterested, restless, disturbed or tired, then stop the reading. It is better to study for short periods, say fifteen minutes than daydream while reading. It is important that students learn to concentrate hard during those short periods. They may take small breaks of five minutes to drink a glass of water while thinking of the questions. Let them do a little spot jogging to get the blood circulation on the go and get back to their seat to finish the assignment. Gradually, as their concentration deepens, their staying power will expand to say, forty-five minutes, and later to much more. Students should never sit to study for more than two hours at one go. After every two hours, they should take a break of fifteen to thirty minutes. It is also important that students should never stop the study session because they have encountered a problem or else they will be reluctant to go back and continue after the break. Do what the movie theatres do – declare intervals at the point of interest. Students should be eager to get back to their seats.

4) Recite: This is the fourth step in the SQ3R method of reading and the most important one. After having read the first section, the student should immediately paraphrase the material as though explaining it to a friend. Reciting the subject matter in their own words helps to transfer the material from the short-term memory to the long-term memory, (recall the art of reeling off jokes). While paraphrasing, a student not only uses the eyes but also the ears and mouth. Involving other sense organs in reading, impacts the memory cells. At times, students could encounter difficulty in speaking out what they had just read. The best way to overcome this is to re-read the material again and maybe again until they are able to recite fluently what they had read. After reading the text, they should write down the points that are difficult to remember. If the material is very dense, students may have to paraphrase each sentence immediately after reading it. Thereafter, as the student picks up momentum reading the chapter, repeat steps two, three and four on each subsequent paragraph or section. That is, turn the next heading into another interesting question, and start reading to answer that question. After reading the text, the student paraphrases what was read (without using the text phrases and without looking at the text or notes) to check for accuracy. They complete the chapter in this way, taking very brief breaks within sections as needed. Students must realise that this is the most important step in SQ3R reading

method. They should spend more time on recitation than on reading because this exercise has multiple long-term advantages:
(1) they learn to run an instant self-check on how they understand what they read,
(2) they learn to spot the weak links in the reading-to-understand chain and improve upon it.
(3) It forces them to think.
(4) As a long-term memory asset, it channels the material into usable format.

5) *Review:* This is the final step of the SQ3R ladder. When standing on the final step, students should look back and review their work. Look back at the questions, answers and notes to see how accurate the paraphrasing or recitation was. Observe carefully the points stated incorrectly or omitted. They should be strict with themselves. In a cool, calm and patient manner they should fix carefully in the mind the logical sequence of the entire idea, concept or problem. When they are satisfied with their accomplishments, it is extremely important that they finish up by writing a brief outline on each paragraph in the notebook. By writing the brief outline, they will do themselves a huge favour as these pointers and notes will come in very handy to refer to at the time of tests and exams.

The five steps of the SQ3R Reading Method, if applied and practised, should result in:
(a) an increase in reading comprehension;
(b) improved ability to identify important points;
(c) better retention of the material.

Students will also discover one other worthwhile advantage at unit tests and exams – the questions will seem familiar because the headings and sub-headings they turned into questions are usually the points their teachers would have used in the exam paper.

Points to Remember

1. The amount of hours spent on reading, ends up as wasted time, especially when nothing is understood or remembered of what is read.
2. Attentive reading demands a mental discipline of being interested in the subject.
3. Reading-to-study is not the same as reading novels and magazines. Reading novels and magazines is recreational reading, while reading to study involves understanding and remembering what is read.
4. Attention to the physical environment is vital to comprehension and retention of what is read.
5. The SQ3R Reading Method is time-tested and result-oriented and is adopted in schools and universities the world over.

10

Accelerate Your Study Engine with Music

Salient Features

Stimulating the brain to focus on studies through the medium of music is indeed a boon for students. The latest neurological research on brain development in relation to music reveals that rhythm, lyrics, harmony and melody stimulate specific regions of the brain responsible for memory, motor control, timing and language. Since music stimulates most parts of the brain in the right and left hemispheres, it can produce powerful emotions of peace, love, sorrow, agitation and more. Results of tests conducted on undergraduates, showed that students exposed to Mozart's Piano Sonata in D major K.448 scored higher marks compared to students who were not exposed to Mozart's music. Tests also showed that not all forms of music enhance brain function; hard rock music does not. Music can be used to enhance linguistic skills and mathematical skills. Learning to musical notes or playing the violin and piano enhances brain functions. Go, blow your trumpet; it will help to accelerate your study engine.

Perhaps you were sitting in a cab or browsing in a bookstore or were you at the bus stand waiting to catch the bus? And, the music came on. As you heard the music, you perked up, so to say. Did it make the foot tap, the fingers snap, the head sway, the pulse quicken? Yes, your brain was emotionally stimulated to respond to the music. According to new research, rhythm, lyrics, harmony and melody stimulate specific regions of the brain responsible for memory, motor control, timing and language.

How does the Brain Process Music?

The latest neurological research on brain development in relation to music reveals that the brain has more than one hundred billion neurones, each developing extensions to other neurones creating trillions of connections. Music enrichment stimulates the formation of connections (synapses) and the growth of extensions (dendrites) in the brain. According to Mark Jude Tramo, neurobiologist at the Harvard Medical School, USA, the brain does not have a specific 'centre' to process music. Music involves many sections of the brain, normally utilised for other types of thinking. It makes sense then that music stimulates and utilises most parts of the brain. Since both, the right and left hemispheres are involved, music has the ability to arouse emotions and memories it actually stirs in these sections of the brain. Music can produce powerful emotions of pleasure, joy, sorrow, peace, agitation and more. At the same time, the brain interprets written musical notes that get processed from the side that is known to handle written words and letters. "This suggests that different emotions are represented in different parts of the brain," said neuroscientist, Anne Blood, who conducted the study at McGill University, Montreal. "You can activate different parts of the brain, depending on what music you listen to. Music can stimulate parts of the brain that are under active."

We Can Learn from Mice

Can music enhance brain function? The answer is yes and no. It depends entirely on the type of music. According to one research conducted on mice (since the brain structure of mice is similar to humans), revealed the following results. A set of mice were exposed to hard rock music for ten hours daily for three weeks. Another set of mice were exposed to classical music for the same period of time. At the end of three weeks, the mice were given a familiar maze to complete. The set of mice exposed to hard rock, found it difficult to complete the familiar maze, while the mice exposed to classical music not only completed the maze but also improved their earlier record. This experiment cautions us on the type of music we listen. Loud, blaring, cacophonic hard rock music not only damages the highly sensitive eardrums, but also dulls the intelligence. The music of Mozart, Brahms and Beethoven have been used in research and proved to be successful in calming the mind, soothing the nerves, healing the body, enhancing intelligence and enlivening a happy mood.

Music Impacts Intelligence at an Early Age

Research conducted by Dr Gordon Shaw and Dr Frances Rauscher at the University of California at Irvine revealed that pre-schoolers who took piano lessons performed 34% better in completing puzzles, map reading and other skills requiring a basic understanding of how we fit into where we are when compared to pre-schoolers who took computer lessons for that same amount of time. This is not to imply that computer lessons are not important in education. The point is that while computers are very effective in the development of eye-hand co-ordination, fine motor skills and other areas of the brain, music is more effective than computers in brain growth.

According to Zoltan Kodaly, a Hungarian philosopher and music teacher, the foetus assimilates data received by the mother. That means education begins nine months prior to birth. By the fifth month, the foetal ears are fully developed and capable of hearing and are able to distinguish voices of parents and familiar music. It is interesting to note that music and voices heard by the foetus before birth leaves a lasting impact. The voices of parents speaking and singing are vital to an infant's sense of security immediately after birth. The elements of music become precious instruments in early education. Rhythm develops concentration, attention and determination. Melody opens up the world of feelings and emotions, while variation in volume and tone-colour sharpens listening.

Music Improves Academic Skills

Wolfgang Amadeus Mozart, born in Salzburg, Austria, was a child prodigy. He composed and wrote entire sections of music at the age of three. He died very young and in debt. His music, over six hundred compositions, was later catalogued by Kochel and is referred to by their "Kochel Number" or "K number". Dr Frances Rauscher and Dr Gordon Shaw conducted IQ tests on undergraduate students using Mozart's music to determine the relationship between brain patterns and music. The researchers chose Mozart's Piano Sonata in D major K.448 for testing because its digitised version closely resembled human brain patterns.

The undergraduate students who were given IQ tests were divided into three groups. One group listened to relaxation instructions, the second to silence and the third to Mozart. The results of the IQ tests were unbelievable. The scores of those who had listened to Mozart increased approximately 10 points when compared to their pre-test scores. Tests also showed that all forms of classical music do not enhance brain function. Researchers point out that Mozart's "Violin Concerti" is an excellent selection because listening to stringed concerts enhances brain activity.

Music Stimulates the Mind and Body

It is a well-know fact that music has the power to calm, the power to comfort, the power to inspire and the power to excite the mind and body. Have you seen the way children respond to music? On hearing music, they spontaneously tap their feet, shake their heads, clap their hands or move to the beat; some may uninhibitedly take off, charged with enthusiasm, moving both feet to the beat, their whole bodies swaying and excited. Unfortunately, music talent is often judged as choral ability or by the ability to play a musical instrument. But music should belong to every child, not just those with talent to sing or play an instrument. Music has to be fully experienced in its many elements. When students tap their toes to soft music and stamp their feet to loud music, they are feeling the music. And, when students allow music to touch their feelings, it makes a much longer lasting impression on their brain cells. Music helps students feel and experience rhythm and melody. When students are exposed to a variety of musical sounds and songs, they learn to appreciate many different beats and at the same time, become familiar with cultural traditions to which the song relates to.

Music Enhances Linguistic Skills

Of all the mediums of expression students learn in life, none could be as universal as music. Music is vital to the development of language and listening skills. Also, it is believed that students exposed to music have a greater motivation to communicate with the world than those who are isolated from it. It is important to expose children to a wide variety of music at an early age – including, pop, classical and semi-classical – and encourage them to sing songs of different languages and cultures, be it *Marathi, Punjabi, Rajasthani, Konkani, Tamil, Malayalam, English* and more. Such exposure will help in developing their music intelligence, which in turn will enhance their linguistic skills. You may want to go a step further with your pre-teens and teens in encouraging them to write proficiently. Encourage them to write down the lyrics of the favourite songs they sing. After they have written down the lyrics, sing the song along with them referring to the lyrics they wrote.

Song writers re-write regional folk songs, at times retaining the original melody and music and blend them into Hindi. Students should be encouraged to use those folk songs to their advantage. How, you may want to know? The tough part is, you will have to make the effort to source out the folk songs in the languages they were originally sung. Then play the original *Punjabi, Marathi, Konkani, German, French, Spanish* or *Cantonese* version repeatedly so that the children are able to sing those songs, too. In doing so, your efforts will pay off handsome dividends; you will enhance your children's linguistic skills. They will develop a natural ability to learn foreign languages by simply hearing the people of the region speak, while the rest of humanity will learn it the hard way, through books and tutorials.

There is a vast difference between learning a new language by hearsay and by learning it through books. The local people of a region speak their language using word-blending, idioms and phrases that are specific to those regions. To 'speak like a native' means that a person speaks a foreign language with the ease and facility of the people residing in that region. A 'native' doesn't speak his language literally; he speaks it idiomatically. When we learn a second language, we usually are taught the language through books, tapes and CDs, and hence we speak it literally, (usually borrowing and translating idioms, phrases and word blending from our own mother-tongue). This sounds *foreign* to a native's ear. But, when children sing pop songs and cultural songs of another region, they are not only entertaining themselves and having fun, but they are also stimulating the language cells in the brain to enhance their linguistic skills.

Music Enhances Mathematical Skills

Come to think of it, you don't need maths tutors to enhance children's mathematical skills; instead, let them learn to play the violin or piano. Better still, let them learn to read music notes. Since experiences help us to understand the world around us in patterns, the nature of the brain's function is to process, organise and interpret patterns. It starts with the patterning of movements. And, very early on, from about five months before birth, the emerging brain starts to pattern its ability to process sound. The hearing system is complete by four months after birth. Movement and rhythm stimulates an infant's frontal lobes, which are the parts of the brain that will enable the child to think and speak. Those frontal lobes grow massively in the first six years of life. By stimulating the frontal lobes during those years, you will lay down the foundation for pattern recognition. Researchers have detected a connection between musical skill and mathematical skill. Both involve the interpretation of patterns. The same area of the brain is active when a person is reading music or playing a musical instrument, as when he is working on a mathematical problem. According to researchers, the musical instruments, which enhance mathematical skills, are the violin and the piano. If you encourage children to take violin or piano lessons, your aim should be that they learn to play the musical instruments, not by ear, but by reading musical notes.

Power of the Arts

Working with toddlers at *Tender Feet Nursery School* – Nizamuddin, for two and half decades has undoubtedly established the fact that the *arts* impact the brain like no other activity. Extensive research carried out by educational scientists the world over also pointed out those students who participated in the arts, including music, art, dance, and theatre through at least one full year were:

- four times more likely to be recognised for academic achievement
- four times more likely to be elected to class office within their schools
- four times more likely to participate in a math or science fair
- three times more likely to win an award for school attendance
- four times more likely to win an award for writing an essay or poem.

Also,
- The arts teach students to be more tolerant and open.
- The arts allow kids to express themselves creatively.
* The arts promote individuality, bolster self-confidence and improve the overall academic performance.
* The arts can help the troubled youth by providing an alternative to delinquent behaviour and truancy, while providing an improved attitude towards school.

Blow Your Trumpet

Students process information in different ways, which means students have different learning styles. Scientists have defined three predominant learning styles – visual, auditory and kinaesthetic. Unfortunately, schools may not recognise the three learning styles and follow a standardised teaching style. Due to this regimented teaching style, some students find it hard to cope with academics. Music could be the answer. Without investing in violin and piano lessons, expose children to listen to musical compositions of Mozart, Beethoven, Brahms, Ravi Shankar and others. During recreational hours and those who listen to music while studying, should listen to soft classical music. It is a good practice to have classical music playing softly at home or in the car while driving. Research shows that people sleep soundly when listening to jazz or laid-back music. It reduces the heart rate, relaxes breathing and induces sleep. The brain responds to music the way muscles respond to exercises. "We found that harmony, melody and rhythm had distinct patterns of brain activity. They involved both the right and the left sides of the brain," said Lawrence Parsons, at the University of Texas, San Antonio. For all those who have a natural talent for music and those who suppress the urge to express themselves musically, go ahead and blow your trumpets; you will only succeed in accelerating your study engine.

Points to Remember

1. Music enhances study skills. Rhythm, lyrics, harmony and melody stimulate specific regions of the brain responsible for memory, motor control, timing and language.
2. All types of music do not impact intelligence. Research points out that hard rock music adversely affects the brain.
3. Music stimulates the body and mind. Fill your rooms and other spaces with soft background classical music at all times. It will improve academic skills, soothe nerves, calm the mind and comfort the soul.
4. Music enhances linguistic skills. Those who find speaking English tedious and difficult, should sing English songs. They may apply the same rule to other languages.
5. Music enhances mathematical skills. Playing the violin or the piano has been proven to enhance math skills. Those learning music should learn to play instruments, not by ear, but by reading music notes.

Epilogue

You live in a pressured world. We all do. You come home from office absolutely drained physically and emotionally. On the way back home, you plan to treat yourself to a hot, warm bath to wash away the day's stress. But that doesn't happen. The moment you unlock the door, without even a breather, you switch roles from that much-admired executive in the office to a disciplinarian, advisor, tutor, cook, cleaner, attendant and much more as you get swept in the eddy of home chores, minus the comfort of the hot bath. This could be your habitual entry home or a rare occurrence. If it is habitual, it means balancing work and family, not only wears you down but also brings on tensions, conflicts and problems. Whether you realise it or not, through your actions and reactions in this muscle-taut, brain-drained state of yours, you set values and standards for your pre-teens and teens to live by.

While you make the transition from office to home, which may not be your finest hour, but it happens to be the peak hour for family interactions, your actions are influenced by your state of mind. Those actions reflect your attitudes, values and all that is important to you. Your habits that exhibit your attitude shape the choices your preteens and teens make. Their ideas, attitudes and beliefs stem primarily from your conduct and interactive styles. To change their ideas, attitudes and beliefs, you may have to change your mindset. The more you spend time with your pre-teens and teens after office hours, the more you will understand the need for change in the choices you make, which affects your career and your family life. Identifying areas of change is the first step toward understanding your current position and helping you to make adjustments to achieve the right balance between office and home. More and more families have discovered that it is healthier to put greater emphasis on living successful and happy lives than simply achieving success at work. If your superiors, subordinates and colleagues interact with a competent, creative, jovial, enthusiastic, lively, spontaneous, supportive person, then your family deserves the same treatment. Why should the family be routinely subjected to a muscle-taut, emotionally-strained, brain-drained parent?

Once you have restructured your mindset, your routine and your habits, you automatically would have reset your goals and priorities. After achieving your targets, say for a couple of months, you would be ready to help your pre-teens and teens make adjustments in their routine and habits.

Occupation

Just as you are in an occupation, your pre-teens and teens are in an occupation. Their job is to study. The more often you emphasise 'your job is to study,' the sooner they will realise their responsibilities and begin to treat their job the way you treat yours. High school is as pressured an environment as any work environment. Both environments have set reporting hours, conferences, meetings, presentations, deadlines, tests and beyond.

Motivation

Make sure your children understand their job description, it makes setting goals and priorities easier. To keep students motivated, you need to show them how to prioritise and set goals. Guide them on what is important, what must be done immediately and what can wait. They feel de-motivated and frustrated from having to do too much all at once. You must be on hand to explain to them the 'bigger picture' and how the numerous 'small pictures' fit like a jigsaw to make the big picture. And most importantly, you must patiently answer their questions.

Build Your Home Team

Without mincing words, clearly communicate expectations around work schedules. Children could be more agreeable to meet expectations when you sit with them to frame the *Term Planner*, the *Weekly Schedule* and the *Daily Timetable*. This routine activity, like no other, will present the 'large picture' as you enumerate the support systems available, deadlines to be met, constraints to be dealt with, like social commitments and preparation for tests and exams. After an open and creative discussion, new alternatives to prioritise the accomplishment of goals may arise and the 'team' feels a sense of engagement from going through the process together.

Keep Communicating

So much for the internet and cellular phones; we communicate with all and sundry throughout the globe, except with the people who matter most to us – our kids. Parents may make a great deal out of attending their children's school functions. But the moment the cellular phone rings, they leave the auditorium, never mind if their child is performing on stage; answering the phone was more important. In many families, communication with members is limited to monosyllables. Worse still, some parents instantly put a stop to all banter and chatter the moment they step inside their homes, ostensibly because they come home "tired" and want "quiet and peace." Just because you have had a raw deal at the office doesn't mean that the whole family suffers your stress. Maintaining good communication with your spouse and children is critical to maintaining a proper balance between office and home. When communication lines are open, atmosphere at home is not only relaxed but you are also able to:

(a) reinforce goals and priorities;
(b) reinforce daily expectations;
(c) meet deadlines; and
(d) sort out problems before they get out of hand.

EPILOGUE

Healthy communication is vital to family health. Anger, grudges, prejudices, stress, tensions and pressures corrode communication lines and vitiate relationships. If you want your children to succeed and lead happy lives, as parents you are duty-bound to provide an environment of joy, not stress, in your homes. When communication flows easily, only then you are able to inject laughter and humour – the most essential tonic to keep the family in high spirits!